UNIX
Shareware and Freeware

UNIX
Shareware and
Freeware

■ ■ ■

By Kevin Reichard

A Subsidiary of
Henry Holt and Co., Inc.

First Edition—1995

Printed in the United States of America.

Library of Congress Cataloging-in-Publication Data

Reichard, Kevin.

      UNIX fundamentals. UNIX shareware and freeware/Kevin Reichard.
          p.   cm.
      Includes index.
      ISBN 1-55828-382-X
      1. UNIX (Computer file) 2. Shareware (Computer software) 3. Free computer software. 4. Operating systems (Computers) I. Title.
      QA76.76.063R4447 1995
      005.3--dc20   94-37067
                                            CIP

10 9 8 7 6 5 4 3 2 1

MIS:Press books are available at special discounts for bulk purchases for sales promotions, premiums, fund-raising, or educational use. Special editions or book excerpts can also be created to specification.

For details contact: Special Sales Director
                        MIS:Press
                        a subsidiary of Henry Holt and Company, Inc.
                        115 West 18th Street
                        New York, New York 10011

CD-ROM in back of the book: The files on the CD appear exactly as they do when distributed over the Internet. Therefore, the author and MIS: Press assume no liability for the software. Users must seek the advice of other users via Usenet newsgroups, or the software authors if problems are encountered.

Editor-in-Chief: Paul Farrell
Managing Editor: Cary Sullivan
Development Editor: Laura Lewin
Production Editor: Eileen Mullin

Assoc. Production Editor: Cari Geffner
Technical Editor: Eric Johnson
Copy Editor: Suzanne Ingrao

■ TABLE OF CONTENTS ■

▼

▼

▼

Acknowledgments

Several people were key in bringing this book to fruition:

- ▲ Laura Lewin at MIS:Press, whose expert guidance shaped this book as well as the UNIX Fundamentals line.
- ▲ Nelson King, whose frequent pep talks kept this project rolling.
- ▲ Eric F. Johnson, whose expert advice is essential. (For those of you who read the fine print, Eric is the technical editor for this book.) Watch for Eric's own contribution to the UNIX Fundamentals series sometime in 1995.
- ▲ The many UNIX enthusiasts whose works are featured in this text. Within most of the **README** files are the names of the hard-working software developers. Send them a line if you find their software of use; quite often your feedback is the only reward these people receive.
- ▲ The many UNIX users whose feedback to earlier UNIX works (*Teach Yourself UNIX* and *UNIX in Plain English*, specifically) led to the creation of the UNIX Fundamentals line.
- ▲ The vendors of the many substances (Wit and Pig's Eye beer, Dunn Brothers coffee) that fueled the many hours of writing and research that went into these series. And thank you, Rykodisc, for reissuing the works of Elvis Costello.

Let Me Know What You Think

Please let me know what you think about this book—why you liked it, why you didn't like it, or ways that it could be improved. In addition, let me know about essential UNIX utilities that I missed, and I'll be sure and include them in future editions. If you have access to electronic mail, you can reach me at:

`reichard@mr.net`

If your communications methods are limited to the more mundane U.S. Postal Service, you can drop me a note care of:

MIS:Press
115 W. 18th St.
New York, NY 10011.

▪ **INTRODUCTION** ▪

Welcome to *UNIX Shareware and Freeware*! This book is an introduction to the vast world of UNIX shareware and freeware.

Shareware and freeware are terms that describe freely available software. Shareware authors explicitly ask for a financial contribution if you find their software useful, while freeware authors hint that a financial contribution would be nice. Both sets of authors have chosen to make their software available to anyone who wants to try it (in most cases, this software is distributed primarily through the Internet, although CD-ROM distribution is an important secondary distribution method).

There are a few misconceptions when it comes to freeware and software. The authors have not given up all rights to the software; by and large they have registered a copyright to the software and have retained all rights to it. And the software really isn't free; as a good citizen of the UNIX world, you should be diligent in sending contributions to those authors who have created useful software. The purchase of this book doesn't absolve you from these contributions. Almost every program has a file named **README** that includes information about financially supporting the software; some others go a step further and include registration forms and more formal licensing agreements. These authors should be rewarded for their hard work—which is why you should send them some money. For the most part, these authors aren't asking for big bucks—typically, they're asking for $35 or less.

What You'll Need to Run These Programs

Obviously, you'll need a running UNIX installation to use these programs. (The exception would be Linux, which *is* a UNIX installation in and of itself.) You'll need a C compiler to install these programs.

For some of the programs, you'll need the X Window System and the accompanying X Window libraries. The X Window System is a graphical interface for the UNIX operating system, and it needs its own set of libraries for programs to be compiled properly. What release of the X Window System is needed depends on the program (**xtetris**, for example, requires X11R5; none, however, requires the most recent release of X, R6). Finally, one of the programs—**mosaic**—requires the OSF/Motif programming libraries. Your task will be to match the resources of your system with the needs of the program, which are usually contained within files called **INSTALL** or **README**. This may seem like something that's beyond the skills of most beginning UNIX users, but selecting and using UNIX freeware is part of the education every UNIX user must go through at one time or another. It's not really that complicated to install this software; it just requires attention to detail and a healthy sense of enthusiasm.

Who Should Read This Book?

This book is meant for the UNIX beginner who wants to expand their horizons past the offerings of their current UNIX system. Most system administrators don't have the time to keep up with the current offerings of the UNIX shareware and freeware world, unfortunately, so many UNIX users are forced to check out freeware and shareware on their own. The type of user that would benefit from this book includes:

▲ Beginning UNIX users whose needs simply aren't met by the tools found within UNIX and X Window, but who lack the financial resources to find expensive commercial software. This might include the documentation expert who's discovered how difficult it is to use screen dumps generated by **xwd** and wants a tool to convert these files to a more usable format.

▲ Any UNIX user who lacks access to the Internet but still wants access to UNIX freeware and shareware.

▲ Experienced UNIX users who need the specific capabilities found in these shareware/freeware tools.

▲ System administrators with limited budgets who are seeking inexpensive tools in response to specific needs.

In short, it's anyone who uses UNIX.

With this kind of audience in mind, this book was written taking nothing for granted in terms of experience and expertise. This freeware and shareware was chosen for its popularity to a wide portion of the UNIX user base; users with more narrowly focused needs should look elsewhere. This freeware and shareware was also chosen for its ease of use; a UNIX beginner should feel comfortable using any of the software covered in this book.

Using The Programs on the Accompanying CD-ROM

For convenience sake, I've included all of the programs covered within this book on an accompanying CD-ROM. This CD-ROM is formatted in the ISO-9660 format, with the Rock Ridge Extensions that should allow it to be read by any UNIX CD-ROM drive. Every program is shipped in C-language source code, and the files are exactly how they were grabbed from archive sites in the Internet.

Because everyone's system is different, there won't be specific guidelines as to installing the software; the steps needed by a Sun workstation user to compile this software will be slightly different than the steps needed by a Linux user or a Cray supercomputer user. As always, check with your friendly system administrator before trying to install these programs on your system. If you're working on a standalone system and want to install these programs, make sure you're familiar with the process of installing software before you proceed. Chapter 9 covers the basics of software installation, but you'll need to put more work into the process, depending on your system and the installation method you use.

Be warned that many of these programs require a little massaging in order to be installed. This is, after all, free software, and by and large the authors didn't do a ton of compatibility testing to make sure that it would run on every system. Most of the software packages contain files called **INSTALL** and **README**; read through these files to make sure that there aren't any known problems before you sit down and curse the heavens after a utility won't install on your system.

Icons

Important UNIX concepts and commands are highlighted with icons from the artist John Bush (who is also responsible for the illustrations at the beginning of each chapter). There are several different icons used:

▲ **Command**, which points out where a UNIX command is introduced and explained

▲ **Note This**, which highlights an important fact or concept

▲ **Take Your Time**, which tells you not to worry about why things work—just that they should work

▲ **This is Technical**, which explains a more technical issue

Conventions Used in This Book

Many of the things discussed in this book will be confusing to you, and sometimes the way books are laid out adds to the confusion. We've attempted to create a very user-friendly book to help you wade through the very confusing world of UNIX computing. Some of the things we've done include:

▲ Commands that are to be typed directly into the UNIX system are indicated by the `monospaced` font.

▲ Keystrokes—that is, keys you press as part of your UNIX system usage, such as the **Enter** key—are indicated by the **bold** type.

▲ Filenames and directories are also in **bold** type.

▲ Machine names and electronic-mail addresses are marked by the *italic* type.

▲ New concepts are introduced and highlighted in *italic* type.

UNIX Fundamentals

This book is one in a series of books from MIS:Press, UNIX Fundamentals, dedicated toward UNIX end users. This series is an ambitious attempt to explain the UNIX operating system in terms the average end user can handle. This is more of a project than you might think—the vast majority of offerings in the UNIX-book world center around advanced technical information for system administrators and UNIX gurus.

If you find yourself curious about UNIX after reading this book, you should check out some of the other titles in the series. The first title, *UNIX Basics*, covers the UNIX operating system from the ground up. Other titles in the series focus on UNIX concepts for DOS/*Windows* users and UNIX communications.

▪ CHAPTER ONE ▪
Introducing UNIX Shareware and Freeware

Freeware comprises a large portion of the most useful software associated with the UNIX operating system. The contributions of many dedicated programmers and users helped make UNIX freeware what it is today. This chapter introduces the concept of UNIX shareware and freeware, focusing on the following topics:

▲ An overview of shareware and freeware

▲ Freeware as replacements for standard UNIX commands

▲ Freeware versus public-domain software and shareware

▲ Using freeware on your system

▲ Coordinating freeware with your system administrator

▲ A summary of the Free Software Foundation

▲ Other contributors to the freeware cause

▲ The reality of using freeware in the corporation

I
▼

A Bargain at Twice the Price

Not everyone connected with the computer world is out to make a ton of money. Indeed, there's a lot of people who think that there should be more openness between computer users, to the point where useful software is given away freely. All that's asked in return is a fair financial contribution to the author.

Sound too good to be true? It's not. The UNIX world prides itself on the megabytes and megabytes of freely available software distributed through various means—the Internet, CD-ROMs, and books like these. This software, commonly referred to as *freeware* or *shareware*, is (for the most part) fully functional software that addressed someone's specific needs at a given time.

Shareware and freeware is much like the rest of UNIX software. UNIX programmers tend to break up tasks into small, easily digested chunks. Therefore, you'll find that UNIX tools—whether they be commands distributed with the operating system or freeware distributed to the greater UNIX community—tend to focus on some very specific actions, and then work in conjunction with another UNIX tool to achieve a greater goal.

Take, for example, the way UNIX treated text processing and editing. Most UNIX users don't use a large-scale word-processing package like *WordPerfect* or *Island Write* to perform their text-processing tasks. Instead, they'll use a text editor to create the text, a text processor to prepare the text for a printer, and the **lp** command to actually print the text.

And this is where freeware comes in. In this process, you can find some freeware tools that improve upon the existing and standard UNIX commands. The previous example could be accomplished by using the **vi** (a text editor), **nroff** (text processor), and **lp** (print) commands. All three commands ship on virtually every version of the UNIX operating system.

However, the process improves when you introduce better tools to the mix. Take, for example, the replacement of **emacs** (a freeware text editor covered in Chapter 2) for **vi**. Now, there's nothing particularly *wrong* with **vi**, and under most circumstances it will do the job.

However, there's no denying that **emacs** will do the same things that **vi** will do, and in addition perform additional tasks that **vi** is not capable of performing. In this case, **emacs** is a definite improvement over **vi**, and as such improves the greater task of text processing.

Similarly, many common UNIX tasks can be improved through the addition of UNIX freeware. This book highlights many of these freeware tools, while the accompanying CD-ROM includes the source code to the programs featured in this book.

What is Freeware?

Simply put, freeware is software given away to the greater computing community. This doesn't mean that the creator of the software has renounced all rights to it—most freeware authors retain copyright of their software, to prevent it from being stolen for commercial purposes. Freeware merely means that the author says, go ahead and use this.

This is opposed to commercial software, where the terms of usage are spelled out in some sort of license—your company agrees to pay the software company for the use of the software.

When compared to commercial software, freeware seems similar to public-domain software or shareware. Public-domain software, by definition, is software cast upon the greater waters of computing, where the author usually doesn't retain any rights—copyright included. Shareware, on the other hand, is software distributed over online services and through user groups, where the author retains ownership of the software, but requires that you send a contribution if you use it. At its best, shareware is "try before you buy"; at its worst, shareware is useful software unfairly exploited by those who are too cheap to register it.

To be honest, there is more overlap between freeware, public-domain software, and shareware in the computer world than most insiders want to admit. Software from the Free Software Foundation (FSF), for instance, is frequently positioned as freeware—yet the FSF is quite clear about expecting some sort of financial contribution à la shareware. Don't get hung up on the definitions of freeware, public-domain software, and shareware; if the author asks for a contribution, by all means send one.

Using Freeware on Your System

You don't need to be a UNIX expert to make use of the UNIX programs on the accompanying CD-ROM.

However, you'll probably need a little assistance when it comes to installing the programs, especially if you work on a larger multiuser system, where a system administrator is in charge. The source code to these programs is included as a convenience to you. If you're working on a home PC, you should be able to follow the instructions that ship with your version of UNIX—Linux, FreeBSD, and UNIXware. However, if you want to install these programs on your company computer and are not the system administrator, you had best check with the system administrator and make sure that:

▲ You are allowed to use freeware on your UNIX system.
▲ There's enough disk space to install the software.
▲ Your system administrator approves of the installation.
▲ Your system administrator is willing to install the software.
▲ You have a C compiler and development system.

In short, your system administrator will make any final decisions about installing this software on your system. In many cases, however, the system administrator (if they do their jobs well) has already installed some or (more rarely) most of the software covered in this book. For instance, if you have a direct link to the Internet, chances are pretty good that any sharp system administrator would have already made *NCSA Mosaic for the X Window System* available to all users.

▼

This is technical

Even if you wanted to install this software on your corporate computing system, chances are good that you lack the proper authorization to do so.

Software in this Book

The software on the accompanying CD-ROM is presented exactly as distributed over the Internet. Its inclusion on CD-ROM is presented as a convenience; if the authors expect a contribution, you should go ahead, register the software, and pay a contribution if you find the software useful. The authors receive nothing from the proceeds of this book, so don't assume that anything was paid to them.

Most of the accompanying software includes license agreements from the creators of the freeware.

This also leads to one of the weaknesses of freeware: the lack of formal support. Don't send this author or MIS:Press electronic mail asking for further support of these applications. The software is presented exactly as distributed over the Internet, so if you have problems, contact the authors of the software with your questions.

The Free Software Foundation

Leading the charge for freeware has been a cadre of dedicated UNIX programmers and users throughout the ages. And the story of Richard Stallman and the Free Software Foundation may illustrate the passion for freeware in the UNIX world.

Stallman is one of the more intriguing and challenging members of the greater computing community. His belief (perhaps summarized too succinctly here) is that software should belong to everyone and not subject to restrictive licensing schemes of any sort. To put his ideas into action, he formed the Free Software Foundation (FSF), dedicated to creating and distributing freely available software tools. The goal of the FSF is to create an entire operating system and supporting tools—all freely available.

As Stallman wrote in his GNU Manifesto (which appeared over 10 years ago in *Byte* Magazine and still is distributed with GNU software):

> *I consider that the golden rule requires that if I like a program I must share it with other people who like it. Software sellers want to divide the users and conquer them, making each user agree not to share with others. I refuse to break solidarity with other users in this way. I cannot in good conscience sign a nondisclosure agreement or a software license agreement. For years I worked within the [MIT] Artificial Intelligence Lab to resist such tendencies and other inhospitalities, but eventually they had gone too far: I could not remain in an institution where such things are done for me against my will.*
>
> *So that I can continue to use computers without dishonor, I have decided to put together a sufficient body of free software so that I will be able to get along without any software that is not free. I have resigned from the AI lab to deny MIT any legal excuse to prevent me from giving GNU away.*

While the FSF has come up somewhat short of its original goals—there's still no operating system from the FSF, per se, though one is promised for the near future—the FSF does offer a lot of very useful UNIX tools. Chief among these is GNU **emacs**, a text-processing package that's much better than most text editors (such as **vi**) shipping in commercial UNIX releases.

▲ **L E A R N   M O R E   A B O U T** ▲

Chapter 2 covers **emacs** in some detail.

The Free Software Foundation also offer several other useful tools, including a C compiler and some replacements for standard UNIX commands.

▲ **L E A R N   M O R E   A B O U T** ▲

Chapter 3 covers other tools from the Free Software Foundation.

This is not to say that the Free Software Foundation is the only organization fostering the growth of UNIX freeware. Many universities and corporations have also been key in the development of freeware (as well as UNIX itself, for that matter) through the years. The popular **gopher** program (used to post information on the Internet) was developed at the University of Minnesota and then given away to the greater computing community—UNIX, DOS, *Windows*, and Macintosh versions alike. And **NCSA Mosaic**, which has done more for popularizing the Internet than any single piece of software, was developed by the National Center for Supercomputing Applications at the University of Illinois-Champaign and (like **Gopher**) has been freely distributed to the greater computing community.

▲ **L E A R N   M O R E   A B O U T** ▲

Both **mosaic** and **gopher** will be covered in Chapter 4, "Freeware Internet Utilities."

Reality Check: Some Issues Surrounding Freeware

When you adopt freeware, you do so at your own risk. There's no formal support for GNU **emacs**—there's no tollfree telephone line to call for support, no one to file bug reports with should you find an error in a program, no one to complain to if the software doesn't work, and no recourse if you don't find the software to your liking.

7

These reasons—as well as some irrational prejudices against free-ware—lead many corporations to forbid the use of shareware and freeware on corporate computing systems. This attitude might be defensible in an all-MS-DOS atmosphere; to be honest, a lot of MS-DOS shareware isn't worth the price of a single floppy diskette. (Of course, there are exceptions. But there's a lot of dreck to wade through when dealing with MS-DOS shareware.)

On the other hand, UNIX freeware carries a rich and proud tradition. Many devoted programmers and hackers (dating back to when *hacker* was an honorable term) have poured countless hours into the development of solid and nifty software. In its earliest days, UNIX itself was freeware: Since AT&T was prohibited from participating in the computer industry, Bell Labs gave away UNIX to anyone interested. And when UNIX development advanced at the University of California at Berkeley, resulting in the BSD distribution, that too was freely given away to anyone who wanted it.

In addition, many useful and groundbreaking UNIX tools were developed with the sole idea of giving them away. The X Window System, a graphical interface for UNIX, was given away to the general public from the very beginning. **NCSA Mosaic**, developed at the National Center for Supercomputing Applications, was freely distrib-uted from the very beginning. And **emacs**, as well as several other tools from the Free Software Foundation, were given away from the very beginning. These are not creaky, amateurish programming efforts—these are among the best tools the UNIX world has to offer.

If you encounter some flak at your organization over the use of UNIX freeware, go ahead and quote the previous paragraph as ammu-nition for your arguments. There's too much good freeware out there for you to miss out on it.

▼

This Chapter in Review

▲ UNIX freeware is software given away to the greater computing community. It enjoys a proud and rich tradition in the UNIX world.

▲ Some of the most useful pieces of UNIX freeware are replacements for existing UNIX commands. For instance, the popular **emacs** text processor is a replacement in some ways for the existing **vi** and **ed** text editors.

▲ Freeware differs slightly from public-domain software and shareware. Freeware is freely distributed, although the author retains copyright. Public-domain software is freely distributed, and the author retains no rights. Shareware is freely distributed, but the author retains rights and demands a specific price for a license.

▲ The freeware outlined in this book is available in source-code form on the accompanying diskette. See your system administrator about installing it on your corporate UNIX system.

▲ Some corporations, particularly large companies, have policies against the use of freeware on corporate computing system. In addition, some system administrators distrust freeware, since it comes with little or no support.

▲ Leading the charge to freeware in the UNIX world is the Free Software Foundation, creators of several popular and highly functional UNIX tools, including **emacs** and the GNU C compiler.

▪ CHAPTER TWO ▪
GNU Emacs

Everybody uses a text editor at some time or another in their computing day. UNIX ships with several text editors, including **ed** and **vi**. However, perhaps the best text editor in the UNIX world is **emacs**. Since **emacs** ships on relatively few UNIX systems, it's not as widely used as it should be, even though it's a great piece of software. This chapter focuses on **emacs**, and topics include:

▲ An overview of GNU **emacs**
▲ Checking to see if you already have **emacs** on your system
▲ Starting **emacs**
▲ The types of documents **emacs** edits
▲ The many modes of **emacs**
▲ Entering commands on the echo area
▲ **Emacs** commands and the **Meta** key
▲ **Emacs** cursor commands
▲ **Emacs** editing commands
▲ Accessing the **emacs** help system
▲ Quitting **emacs**
▲ Learning more about **emacs** through the Usenet

11

▼

Introducing GNU Emacs

Perhaps the most widely used freeware software in the UNIX world is **emacs**, a text editor from the Free Software Foundation (which you learned about in Chapter 1).

Indeed, unscientific polls in the UNIX world indicate that up to one half of all UNIX users had used **emacs** at one time or another.

Emacs is a text editor, and as such it's used to create and edit text files that can either be used as standalone files or as input for other UNIX commands, such as electronic mail. Strictly speaking, **emacs** is not a word processor in the wider sense of the term (especially when compared to word processors like *WordPerfect* and Microsoft *Word* in the DOS, *Windows*, and Macintosh worlds), but this is a nit-picking observation; for the majority of users, **emacs** will serve the greater part of their text-editing needs.

Emacs is also a complicated text editor. It features (literally) hundreds of commands—more commands, as a matter of fact, than some sophisticated commercial word-processing packages. It also includes a programming language, as well as many tools for customization and enhancement.

This is technical

What you think of **emacs** will depend on your views of text editing and text processing. While **emacs** is still a pretty decent text editor, it's somewhat lacking as a complete word-processing tool—like *WordPerfect 6.0 for UNIX*. And while its flexibility was a great thing when first released, **emacs** today bears a close resemblance to *WordStar* or other old MS-DOS word-processing tools, relying heavily on keyboard combinations to perform mundane tasks. (Mouse? We don't need no stinkin' mouse.) You can't see what your document will look like when printed (in other words, **emacs** lacks the WYSIWYG ability: What you see is what you get), so you need to visualize the layout of your file before you send it to the printer.

The lesson? Be prepared to treat **emacs** as a great text editor, not as a lesser text processor (like **troff**) or word processor.

Because the source code to **emacs** is freely available across the Internet, **emacs** has been ported to other operating systems, and it has been subject to different implementations even within the UNIX world. For the purposes of this chapter, the discussion will focus on the straight GNU **emacs** as distributed by the Free Software Foundation (and it will be this version of **emacs** on the accompanying CD-ROM).

The commands described in this chapter may not be exactly the same as those found on your version of **emacs**. Don't worry—not every version of **emacs** is the same. Check your documentation—as described later in the chapter—do check out what specific keystrokes you will use to perform the functions described in this chapter.

However, versions of **emacs** have been ported to the MS-DOS, Macintosh (over the strong objections of Stallman, who views Apple's previous efforts to copyright the Macintosh interface as a heresy), NeXTStep, AmigaDOS, VMS, Atari ST, and Windows NT. In addition, you may be working with a commercial version of **emacs**. Lucid and UniPress Software both offer polished, commercial versions of **emacs**.

▼

This is technical

If you're interested in a full listing of **emacs** ports, Craig Finseth (*fin@unet.umn.edu*) has compiled a Frequently Asked Questions (FAQ) document covering **emacs** implementations and texts. You can ftp the FAQ (entitled **emacs**) from **mail.unet.umn.edu**, in the **import/fin** directory.

▲ **L E A R N   M O R E   A B O U T** ▲

At this point, you may not be familiar with terms like ftp and FAQs. Don't worry. Chapter 4 covers freeware Internet tools, and it also discusses these terms as well as other telecommunications-related topics.

Checking To See if You Already Have Emacs

Even though **emacs** is contained on the accompanying CD-ROM, your system administrator—especially if you have a *good* system administrator—may have already installed **emacs** on your system. To see if this is so, go ahead and type the following command line on your system:

```
$ emacs
```

If you do indeed have **emacs**, it will begin at this point. If you don't have **emacs**, you'll see a message like the following:

```
UX: emacs: not found
```

However, it could be that your system isn't configured to know where **emacs** is stored (in UNIX parlance, the location of **emacs** is not in your PATH statement). There are a few UNIX tools that you can use for further investigation. On some versions of UNIX, the following command line would find **emacs** on a system:

```
$ ffind "emacs"
UX: ffind: emacs not found
```

▼

On most UNIX systems, however, you'll need to use a command line like the following:

```
$ find -name "emacs" -print
UX: find: emacs not found
```

In these cases, **emacs** was not installed on the system. If **emacs** were indeed installed on the system, the **Find** command would return the full pathname of the **emacs** file location.

Some commercial versions of **emacs** run under different names; for example, the Lugaru version of **emacs** runs under the **epsilon** name. If the previous **find** and **ffind** commands fail, check with your system administrator anyway.

▲ L E A R N   M O R E   A B O U T ▲

The accompanying CD-ROM contains source code for **emacs**. However, if you wish to grab **emacs** via the Internet, see Appendix B for details. In addition, Chapter 9 explains how to install the version of **emacs** found on the accompanying CD-ROM for use on your own system.

Starting Emacs

There are three ways to start **emacs**—without a file loaded:

```
$ emacs
```

with a file loaded:

```
$ emacs filename
```

where *filename* is the name of the file you want loaded (**emacs** without a file loaded is shown in Figure 2.1), or with multiple files loaded:

```
$ emacs file1 +100 file2
```

If **file1** or **file2** doesn't exist, **emacs** will create them for you.

```
-----Emacs: *scratch*        11:30pm 2.00   -----All-----
```

FIGURE 2.1 Emacs without a file loaded

When you start **emacs** without a file loaded, you'll be presented with a mostly blank screen with a status bar (called a *mode line* in **emacs** parlance) on the bottom, indicating the name of the file you're working on, as well as other information (the exact information depends on your system setup and the version of **emacs** you're using).

In the case of Figure 2.1, the file—or lack of a file—is indicated by *scratch*, which is akin to some scratch paper; your work exists only in the moment (which **emacs** calls the buffer) and has not been saved to file.

This is technical

Emacs hasn't transcended its roots as a tool for technical users, as shown by the reliance on *buffers* in **emacs** terminology. A buffer, in essence, is the text you're creating or editing. As you work on a file in **emacs**, the file exists only in the computer's RAM, not on disk. If you call a file named **report.1995** and make changes to it, the changes aren't saved automatically to disk; they exist only in the UNIX system's RAM. (A section of RAM is sometimes called a *buffer*; hence, the term in **emacs**.) If you want to make your changes permanent, you must explicitly save the file to disk (a topic that will be covered later in this chapter).

Deciphering the Mode Line

The mode line displays various bits of information, depending on the version of **emacs** you're using. The most important bit of information, however, is the actual mode itself. **Emacs** runs in two modes: major and minor. Within these two types, there are other modes.

You don't need to know about most of the modes (many of them are geared for programmers, such as C mode for C programmers and LISP mode for LISP programmer), but you should know that the fundamental mode is one of the major modes you'll want to use in your work, whereas the text mode can also be useful if you're editing purely text files.

Unless someone has been messing around with your version of **emacs** or you accidentally use a filename extension that launches **emacs** in another mode (for instance, loading **emacs** with any filename with a *.c* extension will cause it to start in C mode), it should start in fundamental mode. If this is not true, use the following command to change it:

```
Meta-X fundamental-mode
```

In this chapter, the combination of a **Meta** or **Ctrl** key and a normal key within an **emacs** command will be joined by a hyphen (-), indicating that the two keys should pressed simultaneously. However, you shouldn't spell out *Meta-X* when you type the command; you should press the **Meta** key and then the second key (in this case, *x*).

▲ **L E A R N M O R E A B O U T** ▲

Your keyboard probably doesn't have a key labeled **Meta**, but this is nothing to worry about—you'll learn about the **Meta** key in the following section.

To change to text mode, using the following command:

```
Meta-X text-mode
```

To change the default mode to text mode (which is a recommended move on your part), use the following command sequence:

```
Meta-X set-variable
```

followed by the **Return** or **Enter** key, then:

```
default-major-mode
```

followed by the **Return** or **Enter** key, then:

```
'text-mode
```

After doing this, any filename extension that **emacs** doesn't recognize will be opened in text mode.

It's very important that you use the hyphen when changing the mode. If you don't, **emacs** will reject your command.

Less important is the minor mode; the important thing here is to start **emacs** in text mode.

When an editor *wraps words*, it stops displaying text at the end of the screen and instead puts the text on the following line. With **vi**, the default is to create long lines of text that scroll off of the side of the screen.

If you want to set **emacs** to always wrap words, it's best to do so in the **emacs** file. See the section "Initialization Files" later in this chapter for details.

Other Modes

Depending on your UNIX experience, there are a few other modes that can be useful. They are listed in Table 2.1.

TABLE 2.1 OTHER MAJOR EMACS MODES

MODE	PURPOSE	SWITCH BY TYPING...
C	Editing C source-code files	**Meta x c-mode**
Nroff	Creating files for input to the **nroff** command	**Meta x nroff-mode**
LaTeX	Creating files for input to the **LaTeX** command	**Meta x latex-mode**
Lisp	Editing LISP code files	**Meta x lisp-mode**

TABLE 2.1 CONTINUED

MODE	PURPOSE	SWITCH BY TYPING...
Outline	Creating outlines, not text files	**Meta x outline-mode**
Screenplay	Creating screenplays	**Meta x screenplay-mode**
TeX	Creating files for input to the **TeX** command	**Meta x tex-mode**

There are even more modes available within **emacs**, but most of the additional modes are of specific interest to programmers.

Enter Commands in the Echo Area

The *echo area* below the mode line (which is not shown in Figure 2.1, since the echo area appears only after commands have been entered into the system) echos commands. When you use a keyboard combination to enter a command, your keystrokes will appear in the echo area. You don't need to explicitly switch to the echo area (as opposed to **vi**, where you must explicitly switch between command and insert modes)—when you enter a command in the system, your input will automatically appear in the echo area. Input in the echo area, used in the course of editing a document, is shown in Figure 2.2.

```
This is emacs in the text mode. Notice how the page
just looks like you're typing in text. There's
not a lot of fanciness displayed here; just a good,
solid text editor.




----Emacs: example.txt (Text Fill)   C2 L2/121 ------
^C
```

FIGURE 2.2 Emacs during the course of editing a buffer

The echo area is also where **emacs** returns error messages. If you were to input something that looks like a command but isn't, **emacs** will beep at you and perhaps flash the screen, indicating the error.

You'll immediately note that **emacs** is on one level easier to use than **vi**: There's only one mode at all times, as opposed to **vi**'s command and insert modes. Therefore, you can go ahead and enter text directly from the get-go. Like **vi**, however, you'll have to press **Enter** or **Return** at the end of every line (unless you've configured **emacs** for wrapping text, discussed previously in this chapter).

As a pure text editor, **emacs** will display only the 95 ASCII printing characters (letters, numerals, and symbols) and the 32 nonprinting characters.

The ASCII file format is the lowest common denominator of computer file formats; files in the ASCII format can be sent to other UNIX commands as input or even to programs on other operating systems.

Using Emacs Commands

As mentioned, entering commands is merely a matter of typing them. **Emacs** assumes that any keystrokes beginning with the **Ctrl** or **Meta** keys is actually a command and should be treated as such.

The Meta Key

One of the more evil aspects of the UNIX operating system—especially for beginners—is its use of a **Meta** key.

Since no one controls UNIX, there's never been one central authority to make sure that UNIX was implemented uniformly across offerings from different vendors. In UNIX's history, each vendor approached UNIX a little differently, both in terms of software implementations and in terms of hardware. A computer running UNIX from Hewlett-Packard, for example, would feature a monitor and keyboard different than a computer running UNIX from Sun Microsystems. (Indeed, different UNIX computers from Sun would feature a range of keyboards themselves.)

However, it was clear that there was a need for additional modifier keys when it came to commands. Thus were born *modifier keys* like the **Ctrl** key and the **Alt** key. But since not every UNIX hardware vendor included **Ctrl** and **Alt** keys on their systems, UNIX designers couldn't assume that the same keys were present on every UNIX keyboard.

The solution was the **Meta** key, which would vary depending on the vendor and the keyboard layout. On PC-style keyboards (which, thankfully, are becoming more prevalent in the UNIX marketplace), the **Meta** key is usually labeled **Alt**.

On older Sun SPARCstation keyboards, the **Meta** key has a diamond shape on it and is located next to the space bar; it is *not* the key marked **Alt**. On other older Sun keyboards, the **Meta** keys are labeled **Left** and **Right**. On some Hewlett-Packard systems, the **Meta** key is labeled **Extend Char**. And on some more obscure keyboards, the **Meta** key really is labeled **Meta**.

The lesson: Check with your system administrator to see what key you should use on your system. If there's an **Alt** key on your keyboard, chances are pretty good that you should be using this key when you see a reference to **Meta** in this section. (If this doesn't work, try using the **Esc** key instead.)

This is technical

In **emacs** documentation, there will be many references to the *key bindings* for the **Meta** key. This is a computer-geek method of saying that a key labeled **Alt** was assigned the functionality of the **Meta** key.

Accessing Emacs Commands Via the Keyboard

Why is the **Meta** key important? Because most important **emacs** commands are entered directly from the keyboard in conjunction with the **Ctrl** and **Meta** keys. For example, **Ctrl-** and **Meta**-key combinations allow you to move around the screen—a throwback to the days when UNIX keyboards didn't feature cursor keys. (However, if your keypad features a cursor keypad and keys like **PageUp** and **PageDn**, these should work.)

With **emacs**, the cursor is actually a *pointer*, and a pointer actually exists *between* characters, not over them. In that respect, individual characters aren't highlighted.

Older text editors used to the cursor to denote the position over an individual character. Newer text editors and most modern word processors use a pointer to designate a specific place in a document.

The handier cursor commands are listed in Table 2.2.

TABLE 2.2 HANDY EMACS CURSOR KEYBOARD COMMANDS

COMMAND	RESULT
Ctrl-A	Moves the cursor to the beginning of the line.
Ctrl-B	Moves the cursor to the left one character.
Ctrl-E	Moves the cursor to the end of the line.
Ctrl-F	Moves the cursor to the right one character.
Ctrl-L	Moves the current cursor line to the middle of the screen.
Ctrl-N	Moves the cursor down one line.
Ctrl-P	Moves the cursor up one line.
Ctrl-V	Moves the document forward one screen.
Meta-B	Moves the cursor one word to the left.
Meta-F	Moves the cursor one word to the right.
Meta-V	Moves the document backward one screen.
Meta-<	Places the beginning of the document at the top of the screen.
Meta->	Places the end of the document at the bottom of the screen.

In theory, these keystrokes are tied to *mnemonics*, keyboard shortcuts that are easy to remember.

For instance, **Ctrl-P** is short for *previous*, so you're supposed to remember to move to the previous line. Of course, this rationale is slightly flawed by the fact that *previous* could stand for previous screen, previous word, or previous letter. This author's experience is to forget about the mnemonics; instead, photocopy Table 2.2 and stick it next to your terminal. Better yet, use the cursor keys on your keyboard.

Searching and Replacing Text

Emacs allows you to search for a specific set of characters and replace them with another set of characters.

To do so, begin by typing **Ctrl-S**, which will summon a prompt on the bottom of the screen:

```
Search for:
```

or

```
I-search:
```

At this point, you'll enter the desired characters, making sure that they are the same case as the characters you're searching for. When you're through, press **Enter**.

To search backward through a file, use **Ctrl-R** instead of **Ctrl-S**.

Changing the Case of Words

A frequent typing errors occurs when you use the wrong case on a word: You mean to type *The*, but you instead type *the*. To fix this, **emacs** has a number of commands that change the case of a word:

▲ To change the case of an entire word to uppercase (*the* to *THE*), use **Meta-U**

▲ To change the case of an entire word to lowercase (*THE* to *the*), use **Meta-L**

▲ To change the first letter in a word from lowercase to uppercase (*the* to *The*), use **Meta-C**

As you might expect, your pointer needs to be over the word to be changed.

Deleting Characters and Lines

If your keyboard features **Backspace (BkSp)** or **Delete (Del)** keys, you can use them to delete characters with **emacs**. In addition, **emacs** also features a whole set of commands that "kill" existing text; whether or not you want to use these kill commands depends on whether you want to do everything from the home row of your keyboard or if you want to actually use the **Backspace** or **Delete** keys. For instance, you can kill lines, regions, characters, and words. Again, the many kill commands are an echo of **emacs'** roots in the day when UNIX keyboards were limited and key-combinations were required to perform many common computing tasks.

Some **emacs** deletion commands are listed in Table 2.3.

TABLE 2.3 SOME EMACS DELETION COMMANDS

COMMAND	RESULT
Ctrl-K	Deletes all characters through the end of the line.
Meta-D	Deletes to the beginning of the next word.
Meta-Del or Meta-Bksp	Deletes backward to the beginning of the previous word.

▼

Transposing Characters

A handy **emacs** feature is the ability to transpose characters, whether it be individual characters or a group of characters.

Remember, **emacs** doesn't know that a word is a word. It only knows that you've typed in a series of characters bracketed by spaces.

Using the commands for transposing characters, by and large, is a lot easier than typing over your mistakes or deleting your mistakes and then retyping the correct characters. For instance, you could be typing merrily along and then come up with this line:

```
My projections shwo that our revenues will be
```

As you type, you didn't notice that you misspelled *show*. You could go back and delete *wo*, and then type *ow*.

A more efficient method—well, a method that uses fewer keystrokes, anyway—would be to move the pointer between *w* and *o*, and then to type **Ctrl-T**. This command transposes the characters on both sides of the pointer.

Similar transposing commands include **Meta-T**, which transposes words on both sides of the pointer, and the combination of **Ctrl-X Ctrl-T**, which transposes the line the pointer is on with the line above it. For instance, the lines:

```
This is a text.
What of it?
```

would be changed by **Ctrl-X Ctrl-T** to the following:

```
What of it?
This is a text.
```

if the pointer were positioned anywhere on the second line.

Saving Your Work

As always: Save early and save often.

To save a file with **emacs**, type **Ctrl-x** and then **Ctrl-s**. At this point, **emacs** will ask you for the name of the file if it lacks a name.

If you want to save your file and quit **emacs** in one step, type **Ctrl-x** and then **Ctrl-c**.

Checking Your Spelling

If you've read the first book in this series (*UNIX Basics*), you've already been exposed to the UNIX **spell** command.

The spell command checks the spelling in a document against a database of correctly spelled words. The **spell** command is pretty limited—the database of correctly spelled words isn't exactly overwhelming in its scope and depth, while it's slightly awkward to use.

Emacs features two ways to check spelling, one building on **spell** and one not. To check the spelling of a individual word, type **Meta-$**; this starts a process to run the **spell** command, which then checks the spelling of the word under the cursor and then asks you to supply a correct spelling if the word doesn't match against a word in the **spell** database. Yes, the effectiveness of this procedure is as limited as it sounds—perhaps even more limited.

The other method involves an **emacs** command called **ispell**. However, **ispell** isn't automatically installed with every version of **emacs**, and it also needs to be installed in an **emacs** configuration file. Check with your system administrator about installing **ispell** on your system.

▲ **L E A R N   M O R E   A B O U T** ▲

Ispell is covered in Chapter 3.

Extending Emacs Commands

Many of the commands listed in this chapter can be extended by adding a numeral to the command.

For instance, the **Meta-U** command changes the case of a word from uppercase to lowercase. If you wanted to extend this command to the next five words, you could use the **Meta-L5** command.

Formatting Text

Emacs is best when creating text files for use by other UNIX commands, such as input for **nroff** or system files like **.profile**. It's weakest when you try to completely format a document using only the **emacs** tools.

Take, for example, the rather convoluted way **emacs** treats tabs. With **emacs**, tab stops are controlled by both spaces and "true" tabs that appear apart a specified distance. If you want to change the tabs on your system, use the following **emacs** command:

```
Meta-X set-variable
```

followed by the **Enter** or **Return** key, then:

```
edit-tab-stops
```

A ruler will appear on the top of the screen, with tabs indicated by the colons (:) above the ruler. To insert a tab stop, press the colon (:) key; to eliminate a tab stop, press the space bar when the cursor is above a colon. You can also use the cursor keys to move the cursor up and down the ruler.

This is technical

As a rule, tabs don't translate very well when you send files from one command to another, as well as from one command to a text processor or a word processor. The way to work around this is to use tabs when you create a file in **emacs**, and then take the tabs out when you are finished creating and editing the document. To do so—*untabify* in **emacs** parlance—use the following command:

```
Meta-X untabify
```

before saving the final file to disk.

Emacs also allows you to do some basic page formatting:

Command

▲ To position your text flush left (as opposed to justified, where the space between words is expanded to fill the entire length of the line), use the command **Meta-X automatic-fill-mode**.

▲ To insert a *page break* (sometimes called a *form feed*) into an **emacs** document, use **Ctrl-L**.

▼

Fonts and Other Formatting Options

To put it simply: **emacs** doesn't allow to specify fonts and attributes like **bold** and *italic*. These attributes may be specified in an **emacs** file (particularly if you work in **nroff** mode), but the actual work is done by **nroff**, **troff**, or some other UNIX command that processes text.

> ▲ **L E A R N   M O R E   A B O U T** ▲
>
> For more information on incorporating formatting in your **emacs** documents, consult Appendix A for a list of suggested UNIX texts.

Printing Options

In a word: none.

You can use the UNIX **lp** or **lpr** commands to print a file created in **emacs**. Or, if you were inserting layout codes in **nroff** mode, you can run the file through **nroff** before sending it to the printer. But there's no method for directly printing a file while working within **emacs**.

Cutting and Pasting Text

You'll find that **emacs** is also more advanced than more common UNIX text editors (like **vi**) when it comes to cutting and pasting text. As opposed to **vi**'s practice of yanking a single character and then moving it elsewhere, **emacs** allows you to move an entire section of text from one place to another.

The steps for doing so are simple:

1. Mark the text.
2. Cut the text.
3. Move the cursor to the point where you want to place the text.
4. Paste the text.

Each step will be explained further.

To mark the text, move your cursor to the beginning of the text you want to move and then press **Ctrl-@**. From there, move your cursor to the end of the text you want to move and then type **Ctrl-w**. The "marked" text disappears. (Unfortunately, **emacs** doesn't physically mark the text that you want to move with highlighting of any sort; you'll have to rely on your memory.)

This is technical

When you run **emacs**, you're also setting aside some system memory for a *kill buffer*. This is a section of your UNIX system's memory that serves only one purpose: Store text after you've moved it. When you move text, you're really moving it to the kill buffer, and from there you're pasting it to the new location. You don't need to worry at all about setting up or maintaining a kill buffer. Don't worry that your text actually disappears—it's merely being moved to another part of the system.

▼

You'll now want to move the cursor to the point on the screen where you want to paste the deleted text. When you do this, type **Ctrl-y**. This summons the deleted text from the kill buffer.

Other Uses for Marking Text

In the previous section, text was marked for the purposes of cutting and pasting it. However, there are many more uses for marking text:

▲ You can mark a section of text and then delete it. In this case, you'd mark the text in the fashion listed in the previous section, but you wouldn't paste it.

▲ You could mark a section and then indent it by typing **Meta-C**.

▲ You could make the case of an entire section either uppercase (**Ctrl-X Ctrl-U**) or lowercase (**Ctrl-X Ctrl-L**).

▲ You could run almost any of the commands listed in this chapter; instead of applying to the entire document, they would apply only to the marked text.

When in Doubt, Yell for Help

Help systems are a rarity in the UNIX world. Too often, UNIX programmers are too harried and hurried to put good help systems in their software. (Indeed, you're more than halfway through a UNIX text and you've not been told *once* about the existence of any online help.)

Officially, the keystrokes for summoning help in **emacs** are **Ctrl-H T**.

This command calls the basic help system, which opens a file listing basic commands. In addition, **Ctrl-H C** summons help for a specific command: After you run the **Ctrl** sequence, **emacs** will prompt you for a key sequence; next, **emacs** will print the command connected to the key sequence. Other handy **Ctrl**-key sequences include:

▲ **Ctrl-H A**, which tries to match a description of what you want to do to a specific command

▲ **Ctrl-H B**, which lists all the key assignments, and

▲ **Ctrl-H F**, which lists **emacs** functions and tries to match your description of a function to a function list.

However, these **Ctrl**-key sequences have not been enforced uniformly in the wider **emacs** world, and you may have to cast around if you want to find the correct help sequence on your **emacs** implementation. To summon **emacs'** online help if the previous keystrokes don't work, use one of the following commands: **Ctrl-H**, the **F1** key, **Esc-?** (which is the way to summon help in the version of **emacs** sold by UniPress), **Esc-X**, **Meta–?**, or **Meta-X**. There's no way to predict which one of these combinations will actually bring up the help system, although **Ctrl-H** is usually a good bet.

The Info Mode

Mercifully, **emacs** also features the functional equivalent of an entire set of documentation that can be accessed at any time.

If you've used UNIX's online-manual pages—accessible by the man commands—you'll know somewhat about the emacs version.

By pressing **Meta-X info**, you'll be put into the info mode (yes, this is a mode, just like the other **emacs** modes you've already learned about), as shown in Figure 2.3.

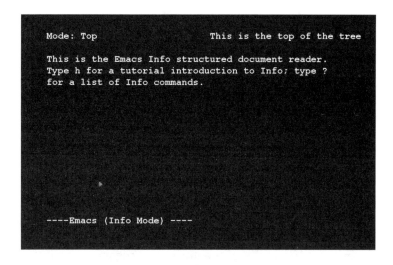

```
Mode: Top                     This is the top of the tree

This is the Emacs Info structured document reader.
Type h for a tutorial introduction to Info; type ?
for a list of Info commands.





        ▶



----Emacs (Info Mode) ----
```

FIGURE 2.3. GNU Emacs in info mode

While info mode isn't exactly hypertext, it is a relatively efficient way to wade through the online documentation. The topics within the info mode are organized by *nodes*, and a menu system is used to navigate through the nodes. You pick a topic, and then you select the number of the node you want to read. There are three levels to each topic, so you essentially go up and down between nodes, moving from topic to topic on the top.

This description makes the info mode much more difficult to use than it really is, as you'll see if you spend a few minutes playing in info mode.

In fact, the best way to learn about info mode is by using the built-in reference tools for the info mode itself. Pressing **h** while in info mode will present a short tutorial on info mode. Pressing the question mark (?) while in info mode will display a list of all the possible commands (and a brief description of each) while in info mode.

Working With Multiple Windows

Emacs allows you to work with multiple files at a given time. To do so, you'll want to open up multiple windows on your screen, each containing a file. (**Emacs** also has the ability to open multiple files, each displayed on a full screen.)

To split a window vertically, type **Ctrl-X 2**. To split a window horizontally, type **Ctrl-X 5**. To switch between windows, type **Ctrl-X O** (the letter o, not the numeral 0). There are many more commands for navigating between multiple windows, but these basic commands should get you started.

Quitting Emacs

As mentioned earlier in this chapter, the **Ctrl-x Ctrl-c** sequence will save your file and quit **emacs** simultaneously. If you have multiple files open, **emacs** will make sure you want to save each opened file.

However, there's a handy way to leave **emacs** without quitting it. Remember: UNIX is a multitasking operating system, which means it can keep track of several processes running simultaneously. You can *suspend* **emacs** while you go to work on other things from the UNIX command line; to do so, you'd use **Ctrl-Z** as an **emacs** command.

Advanced Emacs

There's a lot more to **emacs** than is conveyed in this chapter. For instance, **emacs** can also be seen as a rudimentary programming environment in its own right, supporting a large set of variables that govern its usage.

This is technical

If you know how to program in LISP, you'll feel quite comfortable making changes to your **emacs** configuration.)

While dealing with these files is a topic best left for experienced **emacs** users, the capability is there should you want to dive in.

In addition, the commercial implementations of **emacs** add capabilities, such as electronic mail, not found in the core GNU **emacs**. While these additional capabilities can be very handy, they are vendor specific—which means they won't be covered in this book.

For More Information

There are many newsgroups on the Usenet devoted to **emacs**, the most useful of which are listed in Table 2.4.

TABLE 2.4 USEFUL USENET NEWSGROUPS COVERING EMACS

Newsgroup

comp.emacs

gnu.emacs.announce

gnu.emacs.bug

gnu.emacs.gnews

gnu.emacs.help

gnu.emacs.sources

▲ **L E A R N   M O R E   A B O U T** ▲

In addition, Appendix A lists a number of additional resources if you're interested in further examination and usage of *emacs*.

This Chapter in Review

▲ **Emacs** is perhaps the most popular freeware program in the UNIX world.

▲ **Emacs** is a text editor. As such, it's not really comparable to full-featured word processors like *WordPerfect*. The true comparison is with standard UNIX tools like **ed** and **vi**—and on that level **emacs** truly stands out.

▲ **Emacs** works as a text editor from the start—you type in your text and the characters appear on the screen.

▲ The **emacs** screen is broken into several areas, including a text area and an echo area, where your commands are displayed.

▲ The mode line displays information about the state of the file, including its name, size, and the mode **emacs** is running in. Though there are several **emacs** modes, the handiest would be the text or fundamental modes.

▲ **Emacs** allows you to mark sections of text in anticipation of further actions, which can include cutting and pasting, deletion of entire blocks of text, or basic formatting like a one-inch indent.

▲ This chapter merely touches on the surface of **emacs**. You're encouraged to seek out more information about **emacs**'s many other capabilities. A good place to start is with the **emacs** online documentation.

▲ Quitting **emacs** is a matter of saving the file and then quitting. However, **emacs** also allows you to suspend a **emacs** session while you go on to other work. When you need **emacs** again, it will be loaded into your system and ready to use immediately.

I love GNU-C

▪ CHAPTER THREE ▪
Other GNU Software

The Free Software Foundation is responsible for more than **emacs**, as this chapter shows. Indeed, the FSF is responsible for a wide range of UNIX tools, ranging from replacements for standard UNIX commands to new and specialized tools. Tools covered in this chapter include:

▲ **Gcc**, the GNU C compiler

▲ **Make**, used to make software

▲ **Gzip**, used to compress files

▲ **Bash**, a replacement shell

▲ **Groff**, used to format text

▲ **Netfax**, used as a fax server on a network

▲ Replacements for many standard UNIX commands

▲ **Ispell**, a better spelling tool

▲ Much, much more.

More From the Free Software Foundation

As detailed in Chapter 1, the Free Software Foundation has created much more than just the emacs text editor. This chapter covers some of those additional programs, albeit in lesser detail.

As you scan through this list of software, you'll notice one thing: Many of these packages merely replace existing functionality within the UNIX operating system. After all, most UNIX implementations include some version of **troff** or **nroff**, as well as an assortment of shells (such as the C shell and the Bourne shell). The FSF is committed to creating an operating system that works like UNIX, and these commands fit into that effort. Why use a GNU program as opposed to the implementation in your software? Because the GNU stuff will probably work faster, better, and with more flexibility. In many cases, UNIX tools haven't necessarily been optimized over the years; many times a tool will be introduced with a major revision of the UNIX operating system and then essentially ignored (especially if there are no major bugs within it). On the other hand, the GNU tools have been optimized repeatedly through the years, in an ongoing development project. It's not as though existing tools like **cat** are not any good; it's just that the FSF folks have worked to make it better.

This chapter covers additional GNU tools. In many cases, these tools are for specialized use by a small number of users. You're encouraged to try these GNU tools on your own system, but be warned that you should read through the documentation before you install them on your own system.

Oddly enough, some versions of UNIX make extensive use of FSF software. Linux users, for instance, should already be familiar with the commands in this chapter.

Compiling Programs with Gcc

In theory, you should be able to get a lot out of UNIX freeware without entering the world of programming. The truth is, however, that you will need to compile at least a few of the programs contained in this book. This relates to the biggest flaw with the UNIX operating system: its lack of standardization. When you acquire a DOS, *Windows*, or Macintosh shareware program, you're assured that the program will run, since implementations of these operating systems are consistent across the board.

The same is not true of UNIX. UNIX programs are still dependent on the hardware actually running the operating system to a great extent.

This is technical

Witness the installation of **gcc**. After you've copied the source-code files to your system, you need to then create an actual working version of **gcc**, per the directions. This process involves the tailoring of **gcc** to your specific hardware and operating-system configuration. It's not necessarily an easy process, but one that you will find is worth the effort.

What exactly is **gcc**? It's an excellent C compiler that can be installed on any UNIX system. The latest version of the GNU C compiler supports C, C++, and Objective C (courtesy of NeXT). Obviously, you'll need to know something about programming in the C language before you can attempt to use **gcc**.

Note this

This leads us to one of those many conundrums facing computer-book authors: If you are already conversant in programming, you'll probably want a technical explanation of the capabilities of **gcc**, in order to properly compare it against your existing C compiler. On the other hand, beginners tend to ignore these technical capabilities and prefer to focus on the basic usage. Since there are a host of C programming books on the market—including a planned title in the UNIX Fundamentals series—we'll go with a technical explanation of **gcc**.

As the documentation states:

The GNU C compiler is a fairly portable optimizing compiler, which performs automatic register allocation, common subexpression elimination, invariant code motion from loops, induction variable optimizations, constant propagation and copy propagation, delayed popping of function call arguments, tail recursion elimination, integration of inline functions and frame pointer elimination, instruction scheduling, loop unrolling, filling of delay slots, leaf function optimization, optimized multiplication by constants, a certain amount of common subexpression elimination (CSE) between basic blocks (though not all of the supported machine descriptions provide for scheduling or delay slots), a feature for assigning attributes to instructions, and many local optimizations that are automatically deduced from the machine description. Function-wide CSE has been written, but needs to be cleaned up before it can be installed.

Gcc supports full ANSI C, traditional C, and GNU C extensions. GNU C has been extended to support nested functions, nonlocal gotos, and taking the address of a label.

This is technical

The GNU C compiler has been tested on a variety of hardware (a29k, Alpha, ARM, Convex cN, Clipper, Elxsi, H8300, HP-PA (1.0 and 1.1) i370, i386, i486, i860, i960, m68k, m68020, m88k, MIPS, ns32k, Pyramid, ROMP, RS6000, SH, SPARC, SPARClite, VAX, and we32k) and operating-system (AIX, ACIS, AOS, BSD, Clix, Ctix, DG/UX, Dynix, Genix, HP-UX, ISC, Irix, Linux, Luna, LynxOS, Mach, Minix, NeWSOS, OSF, OSF-Rose, RISCOS, SCO, Solaris 2, SunOS 4, SysV, Ultrix, Unos, and VMS) architectures. Chances are your particular UNIX variant is covered in this list.

Because of the complexity of C programming, you're encouraged to read the manual, *Using and Porting GNU CC*, which is included with the compiler. The manual discusses **gcc** in some depth, but doesn't cover the C programming language in any depth.

This is technical

The **gcc** documentation will refer to files from **bison** as being necessary to install **gcc.Bison**, which is contained on the accompanying CD-ROM, under the filename **bison122.tar**. It also contains its own documentation, which you should read through before trying to configure and install **gcc**.

Using Make

Many UNIX programs use the **make** command to actually create the final program.

This is technical

Not all versions of UNIX contain **make**, however, so the FSF has created its own version of **make** for wider use. As the documentation states:

*GNU 'make' version 3.70 is released. Error reporting is improved and many bugs have been fixed. GNU **make** fully complies with the POSIX.2 standard. It also supports long options, parallel command execution, flexible implicit pattern rules, conditional execution, and powerful text-manipulation functions. Version 3.64 added support for the popular '+=' syntax for appending more text to a variable's definition. For those with no vendor-supplied **make** utility at all, GNU **make** comes with a shell script called **build.sh** for the initial build.*

The library supports ANSI C-1989 and POSIX 1003.1-1990 and has most of the functions specified in POSIX 1003.2 draft 11.2. It is upward compatible with 4.4 BSD and includes many System V functions, plus GNU extensions.

Gzip

Raw source code, as well as many compiled UNIX programs, tend to eat up a lot of disk space. Storing these programs on diskette or CD-ROM, as well as sending these files across phone lines, is problematic because of such large sizes.

To cut down on the size, the UNIX operating system already contains two commands, **compress** and **pack**, used to compress files to a fraction of their size.

None of the programs on the accompanying CD-ROM are stored in a compressed format. These files have already been compressed, to save you an extra step.

▲ L E A R N   M O R E   A B O U T ▲

For more about the **compress** and **pack** commands, check out the UNIX guides listed in Appendix A.

The **gzip** command works similarly to the **compress** or **pack** commands, allowing you to shrink a file or files to a more manageable size. The FSF say that **gzip** is more efficient than **compress** or **pack** in terms of final file size.

However, you're more likely at this time to use the accompanying **gunzip** command, which can be used with any compressed UNIX file—no matter if the file was shrunk with **compress**, **pack**, or **gzip**. To unzip a file ending with .z, .Z, or .gz, use the following command line:

```
$ gunzip filename
```

where *filename* is the name of the file to be unzipped.

When you unzip a file with **gunzip**, don't be alarmed when the original zipped file disappears. In essence, the new, unzipped file replaces the original zipped file. (This is why you should make sure you are unzipping a copy of the compressed file.) For instance, if you wanted to unzip the file **bare.gz**, you'd use the following command line:

```
$ gunzip -d bare.gz
```

When you went to find **bare.gz**, you'd find:

```
$ ls bare.gz
file not found
```

because **bare.gz** was replaced by **bare**—the name of the unzipped file.

Bash, The Replacement for the Korn Shell

The Bourne Again Shell (**bash**) is compatible with the standard UNIX Bourne shell (**sh**). It's also the default shell in some UNIX variants, including Linux.

In terms of features, **bash** is really a hybrid. On the one hand, it's totally compatible with the Bourne shell. On the other hand, it goes past the Bourne-shell capabilities and adds some useful features found in both the Korn shell and the C shell, including:

▲ interactive command line editing

▲ job control on architectures that support it

▲ **csh**-like history features and brace expansion

▲ protected redirection

In addition, it adds several new features not found in the Bourne shell or the C shell, including:

▲ A host of command-line options, mostly controlling how **bash** is started

▲ A ton of variables controlled by the **set** command, including VI (which brings up a **vi**-style editing interface) and EMACS (which brings up an **emacs**-style editing interface)

How useful you find **bash** will depend on your UNIX usage, to be honest.

If you're a casual user and don't make many demands on your shell, you probably won't have a reason to change.

Bash was written with the programmer in mind, and many of the advanced tools in **bash** aren't of much use to many UNIX users. Then again, you may find that one or two of **bash**'s features make it worth your while to switch. Depending on your current situation, this can be painless or it can be a pain. It will be painless if you're using the Bourne or Korn shells, since your current scripts should work just fine.

This is technical

There's one small problem if you're moving from the C shell to **bash**—you must convert your aliases from the C-shell syntax to the **bash** syntax. (If you're unfamiliar with aliases, check with your system administrator.) However, this small problem is directly addressed in the **bash** documentation, as a script contained within **bash**, found at **examples/ alias-conv.sh**, should do the conversion for you.

Why would you switch to **bash**? There are a few good reasons. To begin with: the monitoring of electronic mail. If you're a Type A UNIX user and want to check your mail every few minutes, **bash** contains a number of variables that directly address this issue. For instance, you can tell **bash** to check regularly for electronic mail in a mailbox file specified with the MAIL or MAILPATH variables (the default is 60 seconds, but you can change this if need be by using the MAILCHECK variable). If you do indeed have new mail, **bash** will report this information through a string of your own choosing ("Wake up, there's mail for you") set also with the MAILPATH variable.

Using the History Feature

C and Korn shell users know all about history as it relates to the shell. C shell users can access a list of previous commands by typing:

```
% history
```

at a command line. Korn shell users can do the same with:

```
$ fc -l
```

Essentially, the **history** command line prints out a list of previously entered command lines. For instance, if you've entered the following command lines:

```
cd /letters
ls
cd ..
ls -a
vi letter
```

and then used the **history** command in **bash**, you'd see the following feedback:

```
bash$ history
1 cd /letters
2 ls
3 cd ..
4 ls -a
5 vi letter
```

If you wanted to run the first command line in the list again, you would just list it with an exclamation mark. To rerun the **cd /letters** command line, for example, you'd enter the following command line:

```
bash$ !1
```

followed by the **Enter** key. If you want to run the previous command, just enter the following:

```
bash$ !!
```

followed by the **Enter** key.

In the previous example, five previous commands were used. However, **bash** allows you to retain as many or as few commands as you'd like, using the HISTSIZE variable. To save the previous 20 command lines, you'd use a setting of HISTSIZE=20.

When you quit, the history list is automatically stored to a hidden file called **.bash_history** in your home directory, ready for your use the next time you login the system.

Changing Your Prompt

When used properly, your prompt can be a wealth of information when you're logged in the UNIX system. Other UNIX shells don't offer a lot of flexibility when it comes to customizing the prompt; sure, you can change the characters found in the prompt, and you can enter a UNIX command line **pwd** within the prompt, but you don't have nearly the variables found in other operating systems, such as DOS.

This is not true with **bash**, which offers many options when setting variables inside the prompt, using the PS1 shell variable.

▲ **L E A R N   M O R E   A B O U T** ▲

A fuller discussion of shell variables is outside the realm of this book. See *UNIX Basics* or UNIX for DOS/and *Windows Users*, both part of the UNIX Fundamentals series, for further discussions of shell variables and the prompt.

Indeed, the usefulness of prompt variables is so apparent, it's surprising no other shell designer added the functionality found in **bash**. You can use shell variables to include the time, current directory, name of the shell, the hostname, and more within the prompt.

This is technical

While it is possible to do these things in the C, Korn, and Bourne shells (usually through some convoluted methods; you should see the elaborate shell scripts that implement these variables), it's easy to do with **bash**.

For instance: The following changes the **bash** prompt to include the current working directory (*not* the full pathname, however), followed by a greater-than sign:

```
PS1="\w >"
```

The following changes the **bash** prompt to include the time and date, as well as your username, ending with a greater-than sign:

```
PS1="\t \d \u >"
```

Perhaps the most useful prompt variables are used in conjunction with **bash**'s history features, explained earlier. Within the prompt, you can include the command number and the history number of the command, which decreases the need to use the **history** command regularly.

The full set of prompt variables is listed in Table 3.1.

TABLE 3.1 PROMPT VARIABLES WITHIN BASH.

VARIABLE	PURPOSE
\#	Prints the command number of this command.
\!	Prints the history number of this command.
\<octal>	Prints the character code in octal.
\\	Inserts a backslash.
\d	Returns the date.
\h	Returns the hostname.
\n	Inserts a carriage return/line feed (CRLF).
\s	Returns the name of the shell.
\t	Returns the time.
\u	Returns your username.
\w	Returns the current working directory.
\W	Returns the last element of **pwd** (the basename of the current working directory).

Using Groff to Format Documents

Text formatting is one of the more confusing aspects of UNIX: confusing because it forces you to visualize the layout of a document before you.

As the documentation states:

> *Groff is a document formatting system, which includes implementations of troff, pic, eqn, tbl, refer, the man, ms, and mm macros, as well as drivers for Postscript, TeX dvi format, and typewriter-like devices. Also included is a modified version of the Berkeley me macros and an enhanced version of the X11 xditview previewer.*

As you use UNIX more, you'll learn about **troff**, which allows you to insert formatting commands into a text file. However, the other tools listed here are not as widely known; they serve as add-ons to **troff** and deserve some explanation:

▲ **Pic** is a tool that allows you to insert pictures into a **troff**-formatted document. With **pic**, you define a line drawing (which can be an arc, arrow, box, circle, ellipse, line, or spline) in terms of its dimensions and position on the page relative to other objects. Its greatest utility over the year has been in the creation of flow charts. In these days of WYSIWYG graphics, **pic** seems rather antiquated—but don't let this stop you from trying it out.

▲ **Eqn** and **tbl** allow you to specify equations and tables within **troff**-formatted documents. Both are part of the core UNIX distribution.

▲ The **man** macro package allows you to create UNIX **man** (short for online-manual) pages.

▲ The **ms** and **mm** macro packages are advanced formatting tools that allow you to format letters, memoranda, and other typeset-quality documents.

Other Textfile Tools

The Free Software Foundation also created a series of commands that improves upon common UNIX file-manipulation commands.

These GNU commands include **cat, cksum, comm, csplit, cut, expand, fold, head, join, nl, od, paste, pr, sort, split, sum, tac, tail, tr, unexpand, uniq**, and WC. Most of these commands exist in virtually every version of UNIX, while there are a few, such as **expand**, that are unique to the GNU tools.

▲ **L E A R N   M O R E   A B O U T** ▲

These commands are part of the basic UNIX command set. To learn more about them, check out *UNIX Basics*, the first book in the UNIX Fundamentals series.

NetFax: Sending Faxes From the Network

Setting up a fax on a network can be one of the more painful jobs associated with UNIX usage. However, there's a workable UNIX freeware fax package that, while not the flashiest of applications, performs basic fax functions competently.

The *NetFax* package, developed at the MIT AI Lab and governed by the general FSF license, allows you to send and receive faxes from a UNIX network.

This is technical

The hardware requirements are pretty basic: It requires a Group 3 fax modem conforming to the new EIA-592 Asynchronous Facsimile DCE Control Standard as a Class 2 fax modem. The price of such fax modems have fallen drastically over the last year—it's possible now to find such a fax modem rated at 14.4K bps priced less than $250.

You can approach *NetFax* on two levels. System administrators and programmers can incorporate *NetFax* capabilities into their applications. But—more importantly, as far as the average reader of this book is concerned—it can be summoned directly from the command line as a standalone fax command. This chapter's coverage revolves around that usage.

Installing NetFax

Like most of the programs in this book, *NetFax* should install with the **make** utility and an accompanying **makefile** (there's documentation for this process included with *NetFax*). When installed, *NetFax* actually constitutes several commands:

▲ **fax**, which actually sends the fax from the user

▲ **faxenq**, which enqueues a Group 3 fax job

▲ **faxmail**, which is a mailer interface for sending a fax

▲ **faxspool**, which sets up a spooler queue for faxes

▲ **faxq**, which displays a list of faxes in the queue

▲ **faxrm**, which delete a job from the fax spooler queue

However, *NetFax* is unique in this book in that it also requires some additional software—coverage of which is also included within this chapter and the accompanying CD-ROM.

This is technical

Netfax works with PostScript images; if you send a text file to *Netfax*, it needs to convert that file to a PostScript file, and from there the PostScript file is sent through the fax modem. The answer, as provided in the *Netfax* documentation, is to use the GNU's GhostScript utility (described briefly later in this chapter).

If you haven't installed GhostScript, you'll need to do so before you install *NetFax*. The installation for the GhostScript/*NetFax* combo is a little different than if you were installing GhostScript on its own.

Specifically, you'll need to include a line within the **makefile** that links in the digifax driver (a process explained in the *NetFax* **INSTALL** file):

```
DEVICE_DEVS=x11.dev dfaxhigh.dev dfaxlow.dev
```

Using Netfax

The actual process of using *NetFax* is pretty simple. A queue manager (a **faxspooler** program) must be installed on the host machine where the fax modem is installed. This program periodically scans a queue directory for faxes to be sent. A user can send a fax using the a command line like the following:

```
$ fax options phonenumber
```

or from their mail package, provided the mail package's **aliases** file is configured correctly (not a big deal, but you should check the documentation before making these changes).

The best way to illustrate *NetFax* is to run through a fax session. Let's say a client asked you to fax over a proposal that's you've stored under the filename **proposal**. She gives you her fax number (555-1212). Armed with this information, you send the fax with the following command line:

```
$ fax -p 5551212 proposal
```

This is the bare-boned approach, sending merely the proposal; the only option, -p, tells *NetFax* that what follows is the phone number.

NetFax supports Hayes commands; while the world of telecommunications can be rather murky (therefore, you're excused for not being an expert of Hayes commands), there are a few things you'll need to know about using Hayes commands, mostly relating to dialing out of company PBXes and when using credit cards.

Table 3.2 lists valid characters within the phone number.

TABLE 3.2 VALID CHARACTERS WITHIN THE TELEPHONE NUMBER.

CHARACTER	PURPOSE
0-9	Phone-number numerals.
* # A-D	Auxiliary digits.
T	Uses tone dialing, not pulse dialing.
P	Uses pulse dialing, not tone dialing.
,	Pause, which you can specify; the default is 2 seconds. This is useful when dialing an outside line (such as out of a company PBX, where a 9 might be required for an outside line), or when specifying a credit-card number after the phone number is dialed (for long-distance phone calls).
/	Pauses one-eighth second in dialing sequence.
W	Waits for second dial tone; also useful when dialing out of a company PBX.

There's one other option relating to phone numbers unrelated to Hayes commands, however. When you send a fax, it appears in the *NetFax* queue, in a listing of phone numbers (a list that anyone can access with the **faxq** command). If you specify a credit-card or calling-card number as part of the telephone number, that number will also appear in the queue. To prevent this number from appearing in the queue, put an @ character in front of the phone number.

Of course, you could probably sneak a few more useful options to the command line, involving a cover page and some feedback for you when the fax is sent. A complete set of options are listed in Table 3.3.

TABLE 3.3 COMMAND-LINE OPTIONS FOR THE FAX COMMAND.

OPTION	RESULT
-c	Creates a cover sheet. (More on this in the following section.)
-h *host*	Specifies the host for the fax spooler, if not set with the environment variable FAXHOST.
-m	*NetFax* sends you mail if the fax was delivered or if it failed.
-p *phonenumber*	Sets the phone number for the recipient of the fax. A fax message can be sent to multiple recipients, although each number must be preceded by its own -p.
-r *name*	Specifies a recipient's name on the cover sheet.
-s *name*	Specifies a sender's name on the coversheet; this is not automatically your username.
-S *phone*	Specifies the sender's return fax number on the coversheet.
-u *username*	Sets a username other than your own for usage in the queue.

What can be sent with *NetFax*? Obviously, you can send ASCII files created in something like **vi** or **emacs**. You can also send PostScript files that have been processed with a text processor. Or you can send files in the TeX DVI format. However, don't bother to convert a text file to PostScript or TeX just to send via *NetFax*; in the end, they are all converted to PostScript by *NetFax* anyway.

▼

Receiving Faxes

NetFax also will process incoming faxes through the fax spooler. However, incoming faxes are merely stored in a special incoming-fax directory (**/com/fax/incoming**) on the spooler; there's no mechanism for informing users when a fax was received, or routing it to the appropriate user.

This is technical

This directory can be altered in the **conf.h** configuration file, by changing the INCOMING variable.

In addition, these files are stored as g3-format files, so you must find some way to convert this files to something your system can display.

▲ **L E A R N   M O R E   A B O U T** ▲

You can use *pbmplus*, discussed later in this book, to convert these fax files to another file format. See Chapter 5 for details.

Cover Sheets

One of the nice things about *NetFax* is its ability to create cover sheets. While these cover sheets are rather minimal—listing the date, sender, recipient, and a few other nuggets of data—they're still essential when using the fax in the corporate world.

Information for the cover sheet must be specified on the command line—a pain for those of us who don't live and breathe by the command line, of course. The best way to show this is through an example.

The following command line would fax a text file named **proposal** to Missy Johnson at 555-1212, with a cover letter listing the recipient and the sender (Ted):

```
$ fax -p 5551212 -c -r "Missy Johnson" -s "Ted" proposal
```

The cover sheet must be sent up to include these variables, however.

Setting up a cover sheet is a matter of running another program (**coversheet**) included with *NetFax*; check the documentation for more information.

Tracking and Killing Faxes

As mentioned earlier, the **faxq** command will generate a list of faxes waiting in the fax queue, listing them by file, phone number, and status.

If you decide to kill a fax that's waiting in the fax queue, use the **faxrm** command in combination with the fax's filename.

To kill the fax to Missy Johnson explained in the previous section, use the following command line:

```
$ faxrm proposal
```

Calculating with Calc

The documentation for **calc** says it best:

> *Calc (written by Dave Gillespie in Emacs Lisp) is an extensible, advanced desk calculator and mathematical tool that runs as part of GNU **emacs**. It comes with source for the Calc Manual and reference card, which serves as a tutorial and reference. If you wish, you can use **calc** just as a simple four-function calculator, but it provides additional features including choice of algebraic or RPN (stack-based) entry, logarithmic functions, trigonometric and financial functions, arbitrary precision, complex numbers, vectors, matrices, dates, times, infinities, sets, algebraic simplification, differentiation, and integration. **Calc** also outputs to **gnuplot**.*

Using Gnuplot

Speaking of **gnuplot**: It's an interactive program for plotting mathematical expressions and data distributed by the FSF. It handles both curves (two dimensions) and surfaces (three dimensions).

No, the choice of *gnu* has nothing to do with GNU software, oddly enough.

Assorted Utilities

The FSF offers replacement versions of many standard UNIX tools, including **chgrp**, **chmod**, **chown**, **cp**, **dd**, **df**, **dir**, **du**, **install**, **ln**, **ls**, **mkdir**, **mkfifo**, **mknod**, **mv**, **mvdir**, **rm**, **rmdir**, **touch**, and **vdir**.

> ▲ **L E A R N   M O R E   A B O U T** ▲
>
> These commands are part of the basic UNIX command set. To learn more about them, check out *UNIX Basics*, the first book in the UNIX Fundamentals series.

Finding Differences in Files

The GNU **diff** series of commands replace their counterparts in the core UNIX distribution. However, they are advertised as being faster and more powerful than the traditional UNIX versions.

These commands include **diff**, **diff3**, **sdiff**, **cmp**, and **wdiff**.

> ▲ **L E A R N   M O R E   A B O U T** ▲
>
> These commands are part of the basic UNIX command set. To learn more about them, check out *UNIX Basics*, the first book in the UNIX Fundamentals series.

Replacing Your Shell Commands

GNU tools can also be used to replace standard shell commands, including **basename, date, dirname, echo, env, expr, false, groups, id, nice, nohup, printenv, printf, sleep, stty, su, tee, test, true, tty, uname, who, whoami,** and **yes.**

> ▲ L E A R N   M O R E   A B O U T ▲
>
> These commands are part of the basic UNIX command set. To learn more about them, check out *UNIX Basics*, the first book in the UNIX Fundamentals series.

Grepping Toward the Future

The FSF also distributes faster versions of the **grep, egrep,** and **fgrep** commands.

> ▲ L E A R N   M O R E   A B O U T ▲
>
> These commands are part of the basic UNIX command set. To learn more about them, check out *UNIX Basics*, the first book in the UNIX Fundamentals series.

Replacing Find

The **find** command is used to find files.

However, the **find** command can be confusing for begin-ning users to master. The GNU version offers more options and works faster on larger filesystems.

▲ **L E A R N   M O R E   A B O U T** ▲

The *find* command is part of the basic UNIX command set. To learn more about it, check out *UNIX Basics*, the first book in the UNIX Fundamentals series.

Uuencode and Uudecode

The commands **uuencode** and **uudecode** are used to encode binary files so that they can be sent via electronic mail that doesn't support anything other than straight ASCII data.

▲ **L E A R N   M O R E   A B O U T** ▲

These commands are part of the basic UNIX command set. To learn more about them, check out *UNIX Basics*, the first book in the UNIX Fundamentals series.

Ghostscript

The *GhostScript* utility processes files in Adobe's PostScript language. The PostScript language and the related Encapsulated PostScript (.eps) file format is widely used in the computer world, especially with UNIX and Macintosh computer systems.

Unfortunately, relying on PostScript means dealing with a few unfortunate facts. Adobe controls the PostScript language in the commercial sense; it's not an open standard. Tied directly to that is Adobe's pricing scheme for licensing PostScript, especially to printer companies; this pricing scheme adds a few hundred dollars to the price of a PostScript printer (the exact figure isn't publicly disclosed by either Adobe or printer companies, however). As a result, you can't just use any printer (such as an inexpensive Hewlett-Packard LaserJet) on a network where PostScript files are processed: You're forced to use a PostScript printer.

UNIX hacks hate this lack of choice, of course. The response was to come up with *GhostScript*, which will process files in the PostScript language. The most immediate utility, of course, will be the ability to print PostScript files on a non-PostScript printer.

 Many documentation files in the UNIX world are stored in a PostScript format (they usually end with *.ps*), and the assumption is that you'll be able to send them directly to a PostScript printer with the **lp** command.

This is not a trivial task, however, The PostScript language, when used to format entire documents, also specifies fonts, font sizes, and other page-layout information within the document. When printed on a non-PostScript printer, this page-layout information will be gibberish.

Since there's a ton of page-layout information within a PostScript document, there are many things an interpreter like *GhostScript* to deal with. As a result, there's a ton of documentation that you must go through; especially important are the documentation files relating to fonts and font substitution. You're advised to go through all of the documentation files (in the distribution, these files end with *.doc*) and check through them closely before embarking on any *GhostScript* usage.

▼

This is technical

Be warned that using, implementing and configuring *GhostScript* is not a trivial task, especially if you're using it with the X Window System. X Window has a rather unique way of dealing with fonts, a method that doesn't match the any other font-management scheme in the world. (If you're not familiar with X and its treatment of fonts, you're highly encouraged to check out the books *Using X* or *The System Administrator's Guide to X*, both of which are listed in Appendix X.)

Essentially, you must map PostScript font names to the XLFD (the X method of naming fonts, which specifies the name of the font, its size, and any other characteristics) font names. Luckily, the *GhostScript* creators have included some font mappings for standard X fonts, as listed in Table 3.4.

TABLE 3.4 X FONTS AND GHOSTSCRIPT.

REGULAR FONTS

AvantGarde-Book:-Adobe-ITC Avant Garde Gothic-Book-R-Normal--\n\

AvantGarde-BookOblique:-Adobe-ITC Avant Garde Gothic-Book-O-Normal--\n\

AvantGarde-Demi:-Adobe-ITC Avant Garde Gothic-Demi-R-Normal--\n\

AvantGarde-DemiOblique:-Adobe-ITC Avant Garde Gothic-Demi-O-Normal--\n\

Bookman-Demi:-Adobe-ITC Bookman-Demi-R-Normal--\n\

Bookman-DemiItalic:-Adobe-ITC Bookman-Demi-I-Normal--\n\

Bookman-Light:-Adobe-ITC Bookman-Light-R-Normal--\n\

TABLE 3.4 X CONTINUED

REGULAR FONTS

Bookman-LightItalic:-Adobe-ITC Bookman-Light-I-Normal--\n\

Courier:-Adobe-Courier-Medium-R-Normal--\n\

Courier-Bold:-Adobe-Courier-Bold-R-Normal--\n\

Courier-BoldOblique:-Adobe-Courier-Bold-O-Normal--\n\

Courier-Oblique:-Adobe-Courier-Medium-O-Normal--\n\

Helvetica:-Adobe-Helvetica-Medium-R-Normal--\n\

Helvetica-Bold:-Adobe-Helvetica-Bold-R-Normal--\n\

Helvetica-BoldOblique:-Adobe-Helvetica-Bold-O-Normal--\n\

Helvetica-Narrow:-Adobe-Helvetica-Medium-R-Narrow--\n\

Helvetica-Narrow-Bold:-Adobe-Helvetica-Bold-R-Narrow--\n\

Helvetica-Narrow-BoldOblique:-Adobe-Helvetica-Bold-O-Narrow--\n\

Helvetica-Narrow-Oblique:-Adobe-Helvetica-Medium-O-Narrow--\n\

Helvetica-Oblique:-Adobe-Helvetica-Medium-O-Normal--\n\

NewCenturySchlbk-Bold:-Adobe-New Century Schoolbook-Bold-R-Normal--\n\

NewCenturySchlbk-BoldItalic:-Adobe-New Century Schoolbook-Bold-I-Normal--\n\

NewCenturySchlbk-Italic:-Adobe-New Century Schoolbook-Medium-I-Normal--\n\

NewCenturySchlbk-Roman:-Adobe-New Century Schoolbook-Medium-R-Normal--\n\

Palatino-Bold:-Adobe-Palatino-Bold-R-Normal--\n\

Palatino-BoldItalic:-Adobe-Palatino-Bold-I-Normal--\n\

TABLE 3.4 X CONTINUED

REGULAR FONTS

Palatino-Italic:-Adobe-Palatino-Medium-I-Normal--\n\

Palatino-Roman:-Adobe-Palatino-Medium-R-Normal--\n\

Times-Bold:-Adobe-Times-Bold-R-Normal--\n\

Times-BoldItalic:-Adobe-Times-Bold-I-Normal--\n\

Times-Italic:-Adobe-Times-Medium-I-Normal--\n\

Times-Roman:-Adobe-Times-Medium-R-Normal--\n\

ZapfChancery-MediumItalic:-Adobe-ITC Zapf Chancery-Medium-I-Normal--

SYMBOL FONTS

Symbol: -Adobe-Symbol-Medium-R-Normal--

DINGBAT FONTS

ZapfDingbats: -Adobe-ITC Zapf Dingbats-Medium-R-Normal--

Before the fonts in Table 3.4 will work, you must set them as resources by putting them in a file (~/.**Xdefaults** should work) in the following format:

```
Ghostscript*geometry:  -0+0
Ghostscript*xResolution: 72
Ghostscript*yResolution: 72
```

You must then load the defaults into the X server:

```
% xrdb -merge ~/.Xdefaults
```

Using GhostScript

After you've perused the documentation, you're probably ready to do some work with *GhostScript*. While the majority of the *GhostScript* distribution is devoted to the task of implementing *GhostScript* with other programs (a circumstance that you saw earlier in this chapter, in the discussion of *NetFax*), you can also use it to directly process files for printing.

Instead of going through a lengthy discussion of *GhostScript* usage here, you're encouraged to use the system documentation. In addition, the **gs** command can be used to summon a help system:

```
$ gs -h
```

or

```
$ gs ?
```

Gawk

Gawk is a replacement for the **awk** language.

Ispell

Because UNIX loves to break tasks up into manageable chunks, the strength of individual components can make or break a larger computing chore. This case is never made more plain when it comes to text editing.

Most versions of UNIX include a simple command called **spell**, which goes through a text file and picks out words that don't appear in a database of correctly spelled words. As far as spelling checkers go, **spell** is probably the most rudimentary tool on the face of the earth.

A better alternative is **ispell**, a spelling checker that can be invoked from the command line without a filename, a situation where you must type in a word to be checked:

```
$ ispell
```

More useful is combining **ispell** with a filename:

```
$ ispell filename
```

(where *filename* is the name of the file you want to spell-check) or calling it from within **emacs**. (Check the **emacs** documentation for some tips on integrating the **ispell** spelling checker; if you're lazy, you can run **ispell** directly from a shell prompt within **emacs**.)

After turning **ispell** loose on a file, it will check each word in the file against a dictionary of correctly spelled words. In this instance, **ispell** shares one limitation with **spell**: Both are only as good as their dictionaries.

Luckily, the **ispell** dictionary is much more comprehensive than the rather limited **spell** dictionary.

In one crucial area, however, **ispell** is light years ahead of **spell**. Where **spell** only points out words that don't match its dictionary, **ispell** will also suggest words that are spelled similarly to words not found in the **ispell** dictionary. For instance, a misspelling of aquire will cause **ispell** to suggest *acquire* as an alternative.

And, thankfully, the entire experience is interactive: **Spell** sends a list of misspelled words to the screen or to a file, while **ispell** displays the misspelled word on the screen, along with a listing of alternatives and the chunk of text where the word appears in the file. With the misspelled word and a list of alternatives in front of you, you have a number of choices accessed by the keyboard:

▲   **Spacebar** accepts the spelling of the word for only this instance

▲   **A** accepts the spelling of the word throughout the rest of the file

▲   Choosing the number next to a list of alternatives will substitute the alternative for the incorrectly spelled word

▲   **R** allows you to enter a new word, to be substituted for the incorrectly spelled word

There are some additional **ispell** commands, as listed in Table 3.5.

TABLE 3.5 ADDITIONAL ISPELL COMMANDS.

COMMAND	RESULT
?	Summons the help system.
!	Used to specify a shell command.
Ctrl-L	Redraws the screen.
Ctrl-Z	Suspends **ispell** (not supported on all systems).
I	Inserts the "misspelled" word into your dictionary.
Q	Quits **ispell**.
x	Quits **ispell** without making any changes to the file.

▼

Development on **ispell** took place simultaneously at two different locations. As a result, the **ispell** numbering scheme is slightly screwy, as the Free Software Foundation offers a version 4 of **ispell**, while the originators of **ispell** offer a version 3. Despite the numbering, the version 3 is more recent than the version 4—and the version 3, as grabbed from *ftp.cs.ucla.edu*, is the one contained on the accompanying CD-ROM.

Gnuchess and Gnugo

OK, so not all of the freeware in the world is intended for serious corporate use. But **gnuchess** is a great chess platform, pitting the wiles of the computer against your chess skills. On the other hand, the documentation for **gnugo** clearly states that this version of Go is not yet "sophisticated." **Acm**, a networked X Window air-combat game, falls somewhere in between.

▲ **L E A R N   M O R E   A B O U T** ▲

Chapter 6, "Games", covers **gnuchess** in more detail.

Getting This Software

If you can't use the accompanying CD-ROM, you can grab these files via the Internet. The programs listed here are available on the machine *prep.ai.mit.edu*, which you can login via anonymous FTP, in the */pub/gnu* directory. If you use **ls** on this directory, you'll generate a very large listing. Instead, you'll want to get one of the following files, which contains more information about the FSF and its offerings: **DESCRIPTIONS, README,** and **ORDERS.**

This Chapter in Review

▲   The Free Software Foundation is responsible for a host of useful UNIX freeware besides the **emacs** text editor.

▲   One of the more useful FSF tools is the GNU C compiler, which generates code in C, C++, and Objective C. It can be used with virtually every UNIX variant.

▲   The replacement shell, **bash**, is a usable alternative to shells like the C shell and the Bourne shell. In some UNIX variants, such as Linux, **bash** is the default shell.

▲   The **netfax** program allows you to set up a fax service somewhere on your network. It requires a common and inexpensive Class 2 fax modem.

▲   The **ghostscript** utility allows you to work with PostScript without paying a license fee to Adobe Systems.

▲   The Free Software Foundation also offers a host of replacements for standard UNIX commands—a list too long to summarize here.

▲   Not all is seriousness when it comes to GNU offerings. For instance, **gnuchess** is one of the most popular computer chess program, while **gnugo** and **acm** are interesting games.

▪ **CHAPTER FOUR** ▪
Freeware Internet Utilities

The Internet was built with UNIX freeware, and the best way to approach the many riches of the Internet is through UNIX freeware, such as **mosaic** and **elm**. This chapter covers the many UNIX freeware tools for cruising the Internet, including the following topics:

▲ The link between UNIX freeware and the Internet

▲ Making your own connections to the 'Net via SLIP or PPP

▲ Using **elm** to manage your electronic mail

▲ Using **archie** to track down software and files

▲ Burrowing through the 'Net with **gopher**

▲ Reading the news with popular newsreaders

▲ Some rules for participating in the Usenet

▲ Harnessing the power of the 'Net with **mosaic**

▲ The World Wide Net, in simplified form

Cruising the 'Net With UNIX Freeware

The Internet is all the rage these days. Just browse through your local bookstore and check the number of Internet-related books—over 100 by some counts. While this smacks of overkill—who really needs 100 books on something as simple as the Internet?—the fact remains that the public is wildly interested in the Internet, whether it be as a useful tool for information or trendy barometer of hipness.

The irony is that there's no one definition of the Internet, which is at its basic level an amorphous collection of computers that exchange information via high-speed telephone lines and direct connections. For some people, being on the Internet is a matter of sending and receiving electronic mail from other Internet users. For others, being on the Internet means access to Usenet newsgroups.

For others, Internet access means having the **ftp** and **telnet** UNIX commands available for sending and receiving files from other networked machines. And for others, Internet access means full access to the World Wide Web through browsers like *NCSA Mosaic for X Window*.

The Internet was built on the back of the UNIX operating system. It was the ability of the UNIX operating system to network easily and efficiently that made the first UUCP links possible. It was newsreading programs that made the Usenet popular. And *NCSA Mosaic for X Window* did more than any other single software package to popularize the Internet.

At present there's no one single tool that manages Internet access, unfortunately. Tools for reading Usenet newsgroups, such as **rn**, ship with most versions of UNIX. Standard UNIX commands like **ftp** and **telnet** allow you to connect directly to other machines on the

Internet. And mail-reading commands like **mail** and **mailx** have been part of UNIX from the beginning.

▲ L E A R N   M O R E   A B O U T ▲

Another book in the UNIX Fundamentals series, *UNIX Communications and Networking*, covers the various UNIX tools for Internet access.

However, you'll need to set up your own set of Internet tools for full Internet access—with the emphasis on tools, as opposed to a single tool. For instance, the popular *NCSA Mosaic* is an Internet *browser*, meant for cruising between hyperlinked documents. You can't use *NCSA Mosaic* to read through the Usenet newsgroups, nor can you use *NCSA Mosaic* to read and send electronic mail. As you're learned time and time again in your UNIX education, the UNIX operating system breaks down tasks into small, manageable chunks—and that philosophy extends to UNIX connections to the electronic world.

This chapter covers various freeware tools for accessing the vast riches of the Internet. These offerings tend to be among the most popular UNIX freeware and are growing each day in popularity. Before you can decide which of these Internet tools will meet your needs, however, you need to learn about the various offerings that make up the Internet. This chapter won't cover the freeware Internet tools in any depth; to be honest, they're rather easy to use once installed. Installation procedures will vary from machine to machine—instead of covering installations in this chapter, you should instead check the documentation that is part of each of these programs, found on the accompanying CD-ROM.

This chapter assumes that your company or computer is already connected to the Internet. If this is not the case, the tools in this chapter will be useless. Corporate network connections is something best left to a system administrator; these connections tend to be complex and expensive.

If you're working on a standalone UNIX workstation or PC, you can access the Internet via a high-speed modem (14.4K bps or better) and an account through a local service provider or university. These accounts typically cost $50 per month or less, and they allow you to use the Serial Line Internet Protocol (SLIP) or PPP (Point-to-Point Protocol) protocols for connection. Using these protocols, your UNIX workstation or PC becomes a direct part of the Internet. The details for connections using SLIP or PPP will depend on your arrangement with your local service provider or university.

Some versions of UNIX, such as Linux, include a SLIP program as part of the operating system. Others don't. Your service provider or university may supply a SLIP or PPP software package; if they do, use this, because you'll want to use software that you know will work with your service provider's setup. If not, there are SLIP and PPP tools included on the accompanying CD-ROM. (See Appendix B for details on these programs.) With these programs, you're on your own; installation and configuration vary so widely from machine to machine and service provider to service provider. (Indeed, when you set up a SLIP or PPP account, you'll find that your service provider will be the most popular button on your speed dialer.)

Electronic Mail with ELM

Though frequently ignored by Internet enthusiasts who wax poetic about the riches of the Internet, electronic mail is the killer app that really spurred on Internet development in its early days. If you do only one task on the Internet, it should be electronic mail. With it, you can request information from other resources on the Internet. And with America moving toward a wired future, electronic mail will at some point be an essential business resource.

The UNIX operating system was built from the beginning to enable networking and communications. Early versions of UNIX featured the **mail** command, which was used to send and receive electronic mail.

This chapter won't cover the many issues surrounding electronic mail. For a more complete explanation of UNIX electronic mail, check out *UNIX Communications and Networking*, part of the UNIX Fundamental series from MIS:Press.

The mail tools that ship with most versions of UNIX, such as **mail** and **mailx**, are rudimentary at best. (This isn't true of advanced graphical implementations of UNIX from Hewlett-Packard and Sun Micro-systems, however.) They allow basic management of incoming and outgoing electronic mail.

That's why a host of electronic-mail tools have been created and popularized by members of the greater UNIX community. One of the handiest UNIX freeware mail tools is **elm** (electronic mail), created by Dave Taylor (*taylor@hplabs.HP.COM*) and a host of helpers.

The program **elm** on the accompanying CD-ROM is not exactly the same as the **elm** program Hewlett-Packard includes with recent versions of HP-UX.

The interface for **elm** is shown in Figure 4.1.

```
Mailbox is '/usr/mail/reichard' with 1 message [ELM 2.3]
N 1 Aug 13 Kevin Reichard (15) This is a test - only a test
N 2 Aug 14 Kevin Reichard (33) Proposed statement of purpose
You can use any of the following commands by pressing the first character;
d)elete or u)ndelete mail, m)ail a message, r)eply or f)orward mail, q)uit
To read a message, press <return>.  j = move down, k = move up, ? = help
Command:
```

FIGURE 4.1 Elm in action

To launch **elm**, you'd use the following command line:

```
$ elm
```

As you use **elm**, one thing is apparent: **elm** is pretty easy to use. All of the available commands are displayed, which means you don't need to be mucking around help files to find whether to use **r** or **R** to replay to electronic mail.

Archie

A product of McGill University in Toronto, Canada, **archie** is an attempt to organize the vast offerings of the Internet into a form that can be easily searched. This is not as straightforward a proposition as it might seem—the Internet is already vast and sprawling, and one of the major problems with it is the difficulty for users lacking degrees in computer science to actually find what they need on the 'Net. **Archie** is an attempt to change this.

While **archie** works fairly well within the parameters of its mission, using it still can be somewhat of a challenge— so be prepared to spend some time with **archie** if you want to perform useful searches.

There are three ways you can use **archie** with your UNIX system:

▲ By having an **archie** program available on your system

▲ Through access to an **archie** server via the **telnet** command

▲ Through electronic mail sent to an **archie** server

The second and third options don't concern us at this time (if you're interested in more information, check out *UNIX Networking and Communications*, also from MIS:Press). However, the first option can be accomplished with the **archie** and **xarchie** clients included on the accompanying CD-ROM.

What exactly is an **archie** search? It's a search through FTP sites for a file somewhere on the Internet. Like any computer-based searches, you have some options before actually performing the search. For instance, you can look for a specific program and try to match its name exactly. Or else you can look for a string of characters that's part of a longer filename. You can tell the **archie** server to return the characters with the same case as in your search string, or else you can tell **archie** to ignore case.

Archie actually ships in two different versions: a command-line version (**archie**) and an X Window version (**xarchie**). Both run similarly; the exact details may differ, but the usage is essentially the same. (Both are included on the accompanying CD-ROM.)

Using Archie on Your System

Once you've installed **archie** on your system, you can run it directly from the command line like any other UNIX command or X Window client. The **archie** command is summarized in Table 4.1.

TABLE 4.1 COMMAND REFERENCE FOR THE ARCHIE COMMAND

archie *options string*

PURPOSE

The **archie** command is used to search for a text string among filenames listed with an **archie** server elsewhere on the Internet.

TABLE 4.1 COMMAND REFERENCE FOR THE ARCHIE COMMAND

OPTIONS	
-c	Searches for strings as part of a larger string, with an exact case match.
-e	Searches for a filename exactly matching your search string.
-h	Searches on a specified **archie** server, instead of the default **archie** server.
-l	Returns the results of the search one line at a time.
-L	Returns list of known archie servers
-m*num*	Limits the number of search returns to *num*.
-o *file*	Sends the results of the search to *file*.
-s	Searches for strings as part of a larger string, without an exact case match.
-t	Returns the results of the search by time and date.

The **archie** command sets up a connection to an **archie** server somewhere on the 'Net, performs the search on the remote **archie** server, and then ships the results back to you. Since the **archie** command performs most of the work (as opposed to connecting to an **archie** server via telnet or electronic mail), this is the easiest way to perform an **archie** search. Your **archie** program should connect to one of the following **archie** servers (select the one closest to you):

▲ *archie.sura.net* (Maryland)
▲ *archie.internix.net* (New Jersey)
▲ *archie.rutgers.edu* (New Jersey)
▲ *archie.unl.edu* (Nebraska)

▲   *archie.mcgill.edu* (Toronto)

▲   *archie.uqam.ca* (Canada)

There's some variance as to exactly what **archie** searches for from server to server. Many of the public **archie** servers, such as *archie.internic.net* or *archie.unl.edu*, will look for a search string that's part of a larger string. Therefore, if you want to look for a specific string and nothing more, it's best to use **archie** with the *-e* option, telling it to look for *exactly* the specified string:

```
$ archie -e gcc
```

This command line tells **archie** to look for the **gcc** filename, but not any other filenames that contain *gcc* somewhere in the filename. The **archie** command then performs a search on an **archie** server and then returns the results of the search to you:

```
Host harpo.seas.ucla.edu    (128.97.2.211)
Last updated 09:17 15 Aug 1994


Location: /mnt/fs01
DIRECTORY    dr-xr-xr-x       512 bytes  01:00 26 Feb 1993   gcc

Location: /pub
FILE    -rwxrwxrwx        15 bytes  01:00 27 Mar 1993   gcc

Host jhunix.hcf.jhu.edu    (128.220.2.5)
Last updated 08:50 15 Aug 1994
Location:
/pub/public_domain_software/386BSD/source_tree/usr.bin_
DIRECTORY    drwxr-xr-x       512 bytes  01:00  1 Jan 1994   gcc

Location: /pub/public_domain_software/bsd-sources/usr.bin_
DIRECTORY    dr-xr-xr-x       512 bytes  01:00 30 Nov 1993   gcc

Host interviews.stanford.edu    (36.22.0.175)
Last updated 18:19  5 Aug 1994

Location: /dist/2.6/g++
DIRECTORY    drwxr-xr-x      3072 bytes  01:00  6 Feb 1990   gcc
```

```
Host karazm.math.uh.edu      (129.7.128.1)
Last updated 09:36  5 Aug 1994

Location: /pub/Amiga/comp.sys.amiga.reviews/all
FILE     -rwxrwxrwx      26 bytes  20:32  4 Mar 1994  gcc

Location: /pub/Amiga/comp.sys.amiga.reviews/software/programmer
FILE     -rw-r--r--   4069 bytes  20:32  4 Mar 1994  gcc

....
```

What Do You Do With the Information?

For space purposes, the entire list was truncated. Obviously, this **archie** search was a success, as **archie** displays some machines on the Internet storing **gcc**. One such listing was:

```
Host jaguar.cs.utah.edu      (155.99.212.101)
Last updated 10:32  3 Aug 1994

Location: /dist/hpuxbin/bin
FILE     -rwxr-xr-x   82428 bytes  23:29 18 Apr 1994  gcc
```

There's a host of information in this listing—enough information so you could use anonymous FTP and grab the file from the host **jaguar.cs.utah.edu**. You're told:

- ▲ The name of the host containing the files (**jaguar.cs .utah .edu**)
- ▲ The Internet address of the host containing the files (**155.99.212.101**)
- ▲ The location on the host (**/dist/hpuxbin/bin**)
- ▲ The size of the file (**82428 bytes**)
- ▲ The name of the file (**gcc**)

There's also some other very useful information here, which you may not have picked up on immediately—but information that could save you a vast amount of time as you do your Internet searches.

Because filenames themselves can be highly undescriptive—even when using the longer filenames common in the UNIX world—you sometimes need to play detective and try to divine as much information as possible from the server. In this case, you're obviously looking for a copy of the GNU C compiler, **gcc**, for use on your own system.

This is technical

Take a closer look at the location on the host: **/dist/hpuxbin/bin**. Generally speaking, anything on a UNIX system—whether on the Internet or on your own UNIX system—stored within bin is going to be a binary file (in other words, it's a file that you can run). The *hpuxbin* is a reference to the HP-UX version of UNIX from Hewlett-Packard. Putting this all together, it's pretty clear that the **gcc** file stored on *jaguar.cs.utah.edu* is actually a version of **gcc** for HP-UX. If you're not using HP-UX, this version of **gcc** would be pretty worthless for you. But if you're using HP-UX, then this **gcc** is for you.

As mentioned, the results of the search for **gcc** were quite voluminous. There are two ways to manage this rush of information. You can either limit the number of matches with the *-m* option:

```
$ archie -e -m20 gcc
```

or you can merely redirect the results of the command to a file:

```
$ archie -e gcc > gccreturns
```

There's another tool on a typical **archie** server that you may find useful: the **whatis** command. Because the filenames of many programs can be on the obscure side, some ambitious **archie** organizers got together and decided to associate descriptive keywords with their filenames.

The **whatis** command allows you to search through these keywords, in case you don't know the exact filename of something you're looking for, or are looking for a type of software rather than a specific title. The command then gives you a description of the files that match your query, which you can then search for using the **prog** or **find** commands. The following is a rather simplistic use of the **whatis** command:

```
archie> whatis gcc
gcc                        The GNU C compiler
```

You'll then be presented with hosts that contain this software.

If there are many servers listed, you may find it easier to have **archie** send back the results of the search via electronic mail. (This is different than initiating the search via electronic mail, which is covered in the next section.) To do this, perform your search as described previously. When finished, give the following command to **archie**:

```
archie> mail
```

Gopher/Xgopher

One of the first efforts to harness the immense power of the Internet came at the University of Minnesota, where officials were faced with the problem of cataloguing useful information that could be accessed by the more than 30,000 University of Minnesota students. The solution was **gopher** (a pun on the mascot of the U of M, the Golden Gophers), which would go over the Internet and connect to a remote server. Since **gopher** worked so well at the University of Minnesota, the source code was freely distributed. That lead to a host of **gopher** servers across the world, as well as a host of **gopher** clients created for a variety of operating systems.

Today **gopher** servers are everywhere, or so it seems. You can read Usenet news from a **gopher** server in Great Britain. You can grab software stored on any number of **gopher** servers. A whole host of offerings can be accessed via a **gopher** menu called *Gopher Jewels*. Software can be grabbed just by selecting from a list of available titles.

The accompanying CD-ROM contains source code for both **gopher** (the UNIX command-line version) and **xgopher** (the X Window version). Both work the same in presenting menus as links to other Internet resources. However, they differ somewhat in the look and feel (which should be obvious if you've ever worked on both text and graphical UNIX systems), but the directions in this chapter should apply to both.

The best way to illustrate **gopher** is to run through a few examples. Don't worry if the examples in this section don't match the specifics on your **gopher** program. Each **gopher** is configured a little bit differently. For instance, when **gopher** is launched, it immediately connects to a home **gopher** server. This home server may reside on your else-where on the Internet. For instance, the examples used in this chapter will revolve around the home server at the **gopher** run by the Minnesota Regional Network (MRNet), a service provider in Minneapolis, Minnesota, as well as **gopher** servers connected with the University of Minnesota. Chances are pretty good, however, that your home servers won't be connected with MRNet or the University of Minnesota. Follow this section and note the actions taken to accomplish the task, not the specific menus choices outlined.

Using Gopher

You begin **gopher** either on the command line:

```
$ gopher
```

or by clicking on an **xgopher** icon. If you want to connect to a specific **gopher** server other than the default **gopher** server, you can specify it on the command line:

```
$ gopher boombox.micro.umn.edu
```

Your **gopher** client then connects to a **gopher** server, either on your own system or across the 'Net. After you're connected to the **gopher** server, you're presented with a list of options. For instance, when connecting to **gopher.mr.net**, the following options are displayed in some fashion:

```
Minnesota Regional Network Gopher Hotel
Minnesota Regional Network
Object Database Management Group (gopher.odmg.org. 2073)
Minnesota Datametrics Corporation (gopher.mndata.com, 2074)
Jostens Incorporated (gopher.jostens.com, 2071)
```

This is technical

The exact verbiage will depend on what **gopher** server your version of **gopher** is set up to access, of course. And with a graphical version, you'll see the above augmented by fancy fonts and little graphics indicated whether the line is a document or a directory. With a nongraphical version, you'll have numerals at the beginning of the lines (1, 2, 3, et al) and slashes (/) indicating directories.

Perhaps the best thing about **gopher** is that someone has already gone to a lot of work to make your searches go more smoothly. When you choose an item from a list, the **gopher** server already contains information about the item, and it makes the connection automatically. For instance, in our previous example from MRNet, there are three **gophers** listed with separate addresses. They may or not reside on the same machine—but as far as you're concerned, it doesn't matter. The **gopher** server will do the work of moving to the next set of menu choices. Because of this inter-linking of **gopher** resources, you may end up connecting with **gophers** across the country, and perhaps the world, as you go in search of information.

Using Gopher Jewels

If you're new to **gopher** and want an overview of the vast resources collected on **gopher** databases, you may want to check out Gopher Jewels, a menu item that's found on many larger **gopher** servers.

Actually maintained at **cwis.usc.edu** (a **gopher** at the University of Southern California), but referenced to by many **gopher** servers (the good ones, at least), *Gopher Jewels* is a listing of essential and noteworthy **gopher** resources. As is written in the information statement:

```
Gopher Jewels offers a unique approach to gopher subject
tree design and content. It is an alternative to the more
traditional subject tree design. Although many of the fea-
tures, individually, are not new the combined set represents
the best features found on sites around the world. We offer
solutions to navigating information by subject as an experi-
ment in the evolution of information cataloging. Our focus
is on locating information by subject and does not attempt
to address the quality of the information we point to.

Gopher Jewels offers the following:
     - Over 2,000 pointers to information by category
     - Jughead search of all menus in Gopher Jewels
     - The option to jump up one menu level from any directory
     - The option to jump to the top menu from any directory
     - Gopher Tips help documents
     - Gopher Jewels list archives
     - Gopher Jewels - Talk list archives
     - Other gopher related archives
     - Help and archives searchable (WAIS)
```

When you choose the Gopher Tools menu choice, you'll see a listing like the following:

```
--> 1.   GOPHER JEWELS Information and Help/
    2.   Community, Global and Environmental/
    3.   Education, Social Sciences, Arts & Humanities/
    4.   Economics, Business and Store Fronts/
    5.   Engineering and Industrial Applications/
    6.   Government/
    7.   Health, Medical, and Disability/
    8.   Internet and Computer Related Resources/
    9.   Law/
    10.  Library, Reference, and News/
    11.  Miscellaneous Items/
    12.  Natural Sciences including Mathematics/
```

```
13. Personal Development and Recreation/
14. Research, Technology Transfer and Grants Opportunities/
15. Search Gopher Jewels Menus by Key Word(s)
Press ? for help, q to quit, u to go up        Page 1/1
```

With **gopher**, there are directories and there are resources. In theory, there should be a resource buried somewhere in a pile of directories, but sometimes you must wade through many, many directories to get at a resource.

With this list, you can tell which lines are directories, as they end with a slash (/). You can also tell which lines are resources—they're the ones without slashes.

Your menu may not look exactly like the previous example. For instance, if you're working with a graphical version of **gopher**, there won't be any numbers at the beginning of a line or slashes at the end of a line. Instead, there will be little file-folder icons representing directories at the beginning of lines, and a little magnifying glass in front of the last line of the listing, indicating that a search is performed by the menu choice. (Resources can have several representational icons—files don't use magnifying-glass icons, for instance.)

In this case, you'd use the keyboard's cursor keys (the four keys with arrows on them) to move up and down the menu. When the arrow on the left side of the menu is next to the menu item you want to choose, press the **Return** key. Or, more simply, you could type the number of the menu item, followed by the **Return** key.

Perhaps simplest of all—if you're using a graphical interface, you can move the cursor over the line and click.

Other Popular Gopher Resources

There's not much more to using **gopher** once you've made the initial connection to a **gopher** server. Indeed, you'll learn more by poking around cyberspace and seeing what you find. It's actually pretty easy to connect to remote **gophers** around the world—most larger **gopher** servers contain lists of all the known **gopher** servers in the world, and these lists are typically organized either as one huge list or broken into alphabetical or regional lists.

Many useful and fun resources have been placed on **gopher** servers. Some are listed in Table 4.2.

TABLE 4.2 POPULAR GOPHER SERVERS.

SERVER	CONTENT
basun.sunet.se	Swedish-language **gopher**; answers the immortal question, *Var är Gopher?*
boombox.micro. umn.edu	The repository for **gopher** software.
envirolink.org	Environmental information for activists and others concerned about the environment.
gopher.ic.ac.uk	A large collection of DOS and *Windows* software.
info-server.lanl.gov	Usenet news. (Be sure to use server port 4320 and selector *nntp*.)
internic.net	Information about the various services offered on the Internet.

TABLE 4.2 CONTINUED

SERVER	CONTENT
nkosi.well.sf.ca	Service of the Whole Earth 'Lectronic Link (WELL), which includes articles from *Mondo 2000*, *Wired Magazine*, *Gnosis*, *Locus*, and *Whole Earth Review*; writings from the likes of Bruce Sterling and William S. Burroughs; and links to a whole host of other **gopher** servers.
peg.cwis.uci.edu	A listing of government **gopher** servers.
wx.atmos.uiuc.edu	The University of Illinois Department of Atmospheric Sciences Weather Machine **gopher** server, which provides weather maps gathered from satellite data.

To learn more about **gopher** servers and to see periodic announcements about new **gopher** resources, you'll want to monitor the *comp.infosystems.gopher* and *alt.gopher* newsgroups.

▲ **L E A R N   M O R E   A B O U T** ▲

There are other tools that can be used to extend the power of *gopher*, such as *veronica* and *jughead*. These tools are covered in *UNIX Communications and Networking*, part of the MIS:Press UNIX Fundamentals series.

Reading Your News on the Usenet

There are many UNIX tools for reading Usenet news: **rn**, **tin**, **trn**, **nn**, **readnews**, **vnews**, **xrn** (a version of **rn** for the X Window System), **xvnews** (a version of **vnews** for the X Window System), and **gnews** and **gnus** (both from the Free Software Foundation).

A variety of these tools are included on the accompanying CD-ROM, including **xrn**, **xvnews**, and **rn**. All work similarly: They allow you to read various Usenet *newsgroups* and post articles to said newsgroups.

A newsgroup is nothing more than an open discussion devoted to various topics of interest to the computer world.

▲ **L E A R N   M O R E   A B O U T** ▲

Your system administrator needs to set up the link to a news feed; your newsreader will then be configured to read news from this feed. If you're working with a service provider on a standalone UNIX workstation or PC, you'll need to get the address of the provider's newsfeed and to adjust your software accordingly.

These discussions range from the ridiculous (**alt.barney.dinosaur.die.die.die**) to the sublime (**alt.beer**). As of this writing, there were over 5,000 Usenet newsgroups. Some, such as the aforementioned Barney newsgroup, are on the fringe, while others, such as discussions relating to UNIX and other computing topics, are much more credible in their contributions to society.

The name of a newsgroup follows a very precise pattern, beginning with the general category, followed by the precise topics of the group. When we look at a newsgroup named **alt.barney.dinosaur-.die.die.die**, we can see that the name begins with a category of *alt*, which is Usenet shorthand for an alternative newsgroup. There are many newsgroup categories, and the major newsgroup categories are listed in Table 4.3.

TABLE 4.3 MAJOR USENET NEWSGROUP CATEGORIES

CATEGORY	SUBJECT
alt	Alternative topics, ranging from sex (**alt.sex-.bondage**) to Barney the Dinosaur to supermodels (**alt.supermodels**) to beer (**alt.beer**). These newsgroups tend to come and go quickly; it takes a small group to request the creation of an **alt** newsgroup, and when interest in the groups wane, they are quickly dropped.
bionet	Scientific topics, centering on biological information.
biz	Business topics, where companies are allowed to blatantly advertise their wares. Not exactly the best source of unbiased information, unless you have a technical questions about a specific product.
comp	Computing, ranging from groups for beginners to advanced discussions of computer science.
gnu	Discussions of products from the Free Software Foundation, creators of such popular UNIX tools as **emacs** and **gcc**, the GNU C compiler.
k12	Discussions for schools, ranging from kindergarten to senior high. (Obviously the kindergarten teachers will be more interested in this newsgroups than the kindergarten students.)

TABLE 4.3 CONTINUED

CATEGORY	SUBJECT
misc	Rooms that don't fit under any other subject area.
rec	Recreational topics, ranging from the music of the Grateful Dead and REM to crafts and beermaking.
sci	Scientific topics apart from computer science. A big favorite in the academic world.
soc	Social topics, such as mating rituals or ethnic groups.
talk	The Usenet equivalent of talk radio, with the requisite emphasis on politics and religion.

In addition to the newsgroups categories listed here, there are other minor categories devoted to corporations (such as dec, short for Digital Equipment Corp., a large player in the UNIX world) and regions or countries (for instance, **mn.general** is a general newsgroup for Minnesota-based Usenet users, while newsgroups beginning with *ba* are meant for the San Francisco Bay area).

As mentioned earlier, there are currently over 5,000 Usenet newsgroups. Some, like **alt.barney.dinosaur.die.die.die** or **mn.general**, are of interest to only a small group of Usenet users. Others, such as **comp.unix.questions**, are of interest to a larger group of Usenet users—there are probably many more people interesting in learning more about the UNIX operating system than those wanting to see Barney the Dinosaur die. (In fact, **comp.unix.questions** is a good newsgroup for you to read, since it's meant for UNIX beginners. **Alt.barney.dinosaur.die.die.die**, on the other hand.) To obtain a list of newsgroups, you should first subscribe to the newsgroup called **news.lists**, which periodically lists all of the worldwide (that is, newsgroups not of local interest) newsgroups. You could also consult one of the 100-plus books devoted to the Internet.

How Do I Contribute to the Discussion?

The structure of a Usenet newsgroup is unique, but easy to grasp once you've read through it. When someone contributes to a newsgroup, they are said to *post* news. When you read through a newsgroup, you can read the posts—known formally as *articles*—in the order they were posted, or (if your software allows it) you can read through a *thread* of posts—articles that are posted in response to one another. A thread is simply an ongoing discussion of a specific topic. Depending on your software, you can respond to the post by sending your response to the entire newsgroup (where it becomes part of the ongoing thread), or you can respond directly to the poster via electronic mail.

A Usenet newsgroup is structured in two different ways. Most newsgroups allow anyone to post information and respond to other posts. For instance, anyone can post their favorite method of killing Barney the Dinosaur in **alt.barney.dinosaur.die.die.die**. These groups are ruthlessly egalitarian: You must wade through the meanderings of crackpots to get at the true nuggets of information. Some more useful newsgroups—usually of a more narrow focus and technical or scientific in nature—are *moderated*. Here, you send your post to a moderator, who then decides whether to pass your contribution to the rest of the Usenet.

Some Etiquette for Posting to the Usenet

The Usenet has developed into its own insular world, with some veterans wailing about the infusion of "newbies" (new Usenet users) to their little clique. Don't let these wailings bother you—everyone was a newbie once.

However, there are some steps you should take so that you don't step on anyone's toes.

The Usenet relies on the contributions of everyone to succeed; if you don't participate in a polite way, you're going to alienate some of the folks needed to make the Usenet hum and purr.

Here are some things to keep in mind when using the Usenet:

▲ **Do Unto Others As They Would Do Unto You.** It's OK to disagree with someone—after all, humankind is built upon disagreements. But there's no reason a disagreement need escalate into something nasty. If you're going to disagree with someone, put the disagreement into nonadversarial terms and don't attack the credibility of the other user—just take polite exception to what they're saying. Including a comment like:

```
Well, moron, you're really a swine if you prefer
that crap Bud to Summit Pale Ale.
```

will inevitably lead them to counterattack, and the entire reason for your original post will be lost in the shuffle (even if the other user *is* a swine for preferring Bud to Summit). And the fault will be yours—in Usenet parlance, you are guilty of flaming the other user. Instead, couch your disagreement in this sort of language:

```
IMHO, Summit Pale Ale is a much better beer than
Budweiser.
```

In short: follow the Golden Rule. Don't send the kind of response that would draw your ire if you received it.

▲ **Read through the entire thread before responding.** You may think it's cool to post a response to a question—and indeed, it is. But make sure no one else has posted the same response already. Read through the entire thread before fashioning your response. There's nothing more irritating than reading through 10 messages all saying the same thing.

▲ **Get the FAQ, Jack.** Most newsgroups feature a listing of Frequently Asked Questions, or FAQs. They usually contain the answers to your "dumb" questions. (See "Just the FAQs, Ma'am," later in this chapter.)

▲ **Don't expect immediate answers.** Usenet news doesn't travel as fast as electronic mail. As explained in the previous chapter, some system administrators take advantage of lower long-distance rates and grab the Usenet feed in the middle of the night. Your query may not be passed along to the rest of the Usenet until then, and it may take a few days before the entire Usenet has seen your query. Add the few days necessary to get a response back to you, and you may end up waiting a week before anyone responds to your "hot" query.

▲ **Don't expect others to do your work for you.** If you're in college and need advice with a problem, don't expect others to solve your problem for you. (Similarly, don't bug authors of programming books when you've got an important project due and you need someone to solve your mistakes. You'd be amazed how often this happens.) Do your own legwork. If you're still having problems, then ask others for help.

▲ **Be precise in your queries.** The vaguer the question, the less likely you're going to get a usable response. Don't ask someone to explain how to program in C, or to summarize the works of Henry James in 40 words.

▲ **Take it easy with the quoting.** Don't automatically include the entire text—something that this software allows you to do. Take the time to edit down the original article to the section or sections you're responding to, while eliminating other portions.

▲ **Make sure your signature says something.** Many UNIX newsreaders allow you to set up a signature file (the exact file depends on the newsreader, but **.signature** is a common filename), which is merely an ASCII file that contains information about you, as in the following:

```
================================================
Kevin Reichard                reichard@mr.net

1677 Laurel Av.          kreichard@mcimail.com

St. Paul, MN 55104          CServe: 73670,3422
================================================
```

Some people go to great and elaborate lengths with their signature file, including their company, its full address, their many e-mail addresses, and a huge quote apropos of nothing. In many of these cases, these self-centered users have signatures that are larger than the text of their message! Again, keep it short and sweet when it comes to signature files.

Just the FAQs, Ma'am

As Usenet users tired of answering the same questions time and time again, they responded by appointing someone in charge of the Frequently Asked Questions (FAQs) that are posted periodically to Usenet newsgroups. A sample FAQ from the **alt.buddha.short.fat.guy** newsgroup is shown in Figure 4.2.

```
From news.answers Wed Sep 14 13:00:52 1994
From: Alf the Poet <piz!alf@afs.com>
Subject: alt.buddha.short.fat.guy Frequently Asked Questions
(FAQ)
Followup-To: alt.buddha.short.fat.guy
Summary: Celebrating a prominent religious figure who really
exists, plus El Dupree.

Archive-name: alt-buddha-short-fat-guy-faq

This is the Frequently Asked Questions list for
alt.buddha.short.fat.guy.
It is posted infrequently enough to be frustrating but often
enough to be annoying. Relax. Have a cigar.

A friend writes:
>Yes, you are correct, it is annoying and it is not funny. It
>displays a profound ignorance of Buddhism and a remarkable
```

>insensitivity to the millions of people who practice it.

As we said, "Relax. Have a cigar." More precisely, "Mu."

Contents

Note that vertical bars in column 75 indicate lines that have
been added or changed since that last posting of the FAQ.
Deleted lines are indicated by, well, being deleted.

Send questions for inclusion in this list to Alf@afs.com.

****
Section 1. Getting Started
****

1-1.   Does this newsgroup have a FAQ list?

         Yes.

1-2.   How can I get it?

         Apparently, you don't.

1-3.   Does this newsgroup have a purpose?

         Yes.

1-4.   Which is?

         See question 1-2.

1-5.   Is this an actual newsgroup, or is my system being toyed
        with?

        Yes, and yes.

1-6.   Shouldn't you change the name? THE Buddha wasn't short
        or fat. Besides, it's insulting to real Buddhists.

        See questions 2-4, 4-3, 1-6, and Appendix B.

1-7.   For people who claim to be buddhists, you guys are
        awfully X.

        What? Irreverent? Silly? Disrespectful? Intelligent?
        Strong? Handsome? Shapely? Turquoise? What??!!

1-8.   Arrrggghhh! Fine, then, do what you like.

        Heh. Don't tell me what to do!

```
**********************
Section 2.  The Buddha
**********************
```

2-1.   Who was the Buddha?

        The Buddha, originally called Gautama, was a young
        Ksatriya of comfortable means who became disillusioned
        with his bourgeois existence and set out to find himself.
        He adopted an austere way of life, even abandoning his
        Doors tapes - certainly not standard procedure for those
        on similar quests. Eventually, he achieved enlighten-
        ment, whereupon he became known as "The Buddha," "The
        Enlightened One," or, to his friends, "Budd Light."

2-2.   Isn't it silly having so many names for one person?

        I'm sorry. I can't argue unless you've paid.

2-3.   Wait, what about the "Buddah"?

        He spends his time hanging out with Ghandi in New Dheli.
        Munching on gerkhins, no doubt.

2-4.   Is the purpose of this newsgroup to insult the Buddha?

No. However, since the last thing the Buddha wanted was
veneration, perhaps we are insulting him by not insulting him. You have deeply troubled us.

FIGURE 4.2 The beginning of the alt.buddha.short.fat.guy FAQ

Not all of the Usenet FAQs are this much fun, of course.

As a UNIX beginner, you may want to check out the FAQ periodically posted to **comp.unix.questions**, a newsgroup devoted to
UNIX beginners and their many questions.

Making Sense with Mosaic

Even if you're not connected to the Internet, you've probably heard of
NCSA Mosaic for X Window or one of several commercial offerings
based on *Mosaic*. Developed by the National Center for Supercomputing
Applications (NCSA), *Mosaic* is designed as a hypertext browser.

For this to mean anything, however, you'll need to know a
little about the various offerings of the Internet when it
comes to hypertext and the World Wide Web.

These are the tools that allow vast amounts of digitized data to be collected and catalogued—and, perhaps most importantly, organized in
such a way so that it can be easily found by computer users like yourself. One of the biggest problems with the Internet in the past has been

the lack of organization when it came to information—neat things may have been available on the Internet, but few people knew how to access them.

The World Wide Web

The World Wide Web, or WWW, is perhaps one of the most important computing efforts of the last 50 years. Created and overseen by CERN, the European Laboratory for Particle Physics), the WWW is an attempt to create a worldwide distributed hypermedia system. It's also why most Internet users are bullish on the future of the Internet as a useful and exciting way to distribute information around the world.

A *distributed hypermedia system?* In English, this means that Internet documents can contain links to other Internet documents. In this case, an Internet document can be a file on an FTP site (the sort of thing you used **archie** to search for earlier in this chapter), the contents of a Usenet newsgroup, the result of a WAIS search, or a **telnet** connection to another Internet-connected machine.

In short, the format of the document shouldn't matter if you're on the WWW; you should be able to move between any Internet documents without having to use multiple tools to access them. And everything should be transparent to the user, who shouldn't have to care if a document is stored on an FTP site, a **gopher** server, or something else.

In addition, the design of WWW documents is unlike anything else on the Internet. Thanks to the assumption that most Internet browsers will contain some basic fonts, most WW documents look more like "real" documents (as in something you would see in a book or magazine) than a page of text on a computer screen. In addition, most WWW browsers contain the ability to display graphics, which are sent in compressed form over the Internet and then uncompressed on your machine. (You'll see some examples of attractive WWW graphics later in this chapter.)

The best way to illustrate these WWW documents and links is to examine a typical WWW site on the Internet. The most useful WWW pages, at this point in the Web's evolution, involve technical information from the likes of Sun Microsystems and SCO. Figure 4.3 shows the home page to the Sun Microsystems WWW server at *http://www.sun.com.*

FIGURE 4.3 The home page to the Sun WWW server

Figure 4.3 shows the starting point to Sun's many resources available through the Web. By clicking on one of the many attractive icons, you can move to another document linked to the home page. For instance, clicking on **Service and Support** gets you to the page shown in Figure 4.4. (By the way, the black-and-white renderings in this chapter don't do justice to the attractiveness of these color Sun pages.)

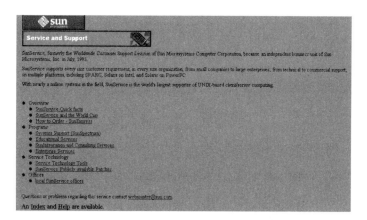

FIGURE 4.4 The Service and Support page from Sun

The approach taken by Sun is pretty straightforward: Corporate resources are listed in a series of menus. You can move between WWW pages by clicking on a highlighted area of text.

To get to a WWW site, you first need to have the document's Uniform Resource Locator, or URL. URLs come in a variety of formats, but they all look basically the same; the differences lie in the type of the document they represent. The range of URLs and their formats are summarized in Table 4.4.

TABLE 4.4 URL FORMATS AND THEIR MEANINGS, COURTESY OF THE WWW FAQ

FORMAT	REPRESENTS
file://wuarchive.wustl.edu/ mirrors/msdos/graphics/gifkit.zip	File at an FTP site.
ftp: //wuarchive.wustl.edu/mirrors	FTP site.
http:info.cern.ch:80/default.html	WWW site.
news:alt.hypertext	Usenet newsgroup.
telnet://dra.com	**Telnet** connection to Internet-connected server.

Getting on the WWW

Your system administrator needs to handle the details of getting your company connected to the World Wide Web. Generally speaking, the best method is through a direct connection to the Internet, which can then be accessed on your UNIX by a browser like *Viola, Mosaic,* or *Lynx.*

UNIX users have a wide variety of web browsers available:

▲ *NCSA Mosaic for the X Window System*

▲ *tkWWW Browser/Editor for X11* (written in the Tk language)

▲ *MidasWWW* (runs under X)

▲ *Viola for X*

▲ *Chimera*

▲ *Lynx* (text only)

▲ *perlWWW* (a text-only browser written in the perl language)

All of these tools are included on the accompanying CD-ROM, and each works a little differently; if one browser doesn't fit your needs or doesn't feel comfortable, feel free to scrap it and adopt another browser. However, for the purposes of this discussion, we'll focus on *NCSA Mosaic for the X Window System.*

Mosaic does not ship in a text-driven version; it only ships in versions compiled for use in the X Window System. If you are not running the X Window System, you'll need to use a text-oriented browser, such as *Lynx.*

Using Mosaic

The most popular of these browsers is *NCSA Mosaic for the X Window System* (which will be referred to for the remainder of this chapter as

mosaic, since that's the command you'll use to launch it) from the National Center for Supercomputing Applications. Indeed, if there's one tool that has popularized the concept of the WWW, it's **mosaic**.

Mosaic comes in several different versions. The NCSA distributes **mosaic** in compiled form for various architectures; however, the CD-ROM contains only the source code. You will have to do some searching on the 'Net to find:

- ▲ Sun 4, SunOS 4.1.x
- ▲ Sun 4, SunOS 4.1.x, no DNS
- ▲ Silicon Graphics Irix 4.x
- ▲ IBM RS/6000, AIX 3.2
- ▲ DEC MIPS Ultrix
- ▲ DEC Alpha AXP, OSF/1
- ▲ H-P 9000/700, HP-UX 9.x
- ▲ Linux
- ▲ UnixWare
- ▲ SCO OpenDesktop
- ▲ Apple A/UX

Just because a version of **mosaic** has been compiled for your system doesn't mean that it will run with no configuration on your end. For instance, installing the version of **mosaic** for UnixWare involved some system-configuration issues, including font allocations.

If you plan on using it, the version of **Mosaic** on the CD-ROM, be warned that you'll need the complete libraries for OSF/Motif 1.1 installed on your system. (The runtime versions, on the other hand, do not have this requirement.)

You launch **mosaic** with the following command line:

```
$ mosaic
```

This takes you to a default URL, or *home page*, which you connect to every time you launch **mosaic**. If you want to connect to a different URL, you can use a command line like the following:

```
$ mosaic http://www.infonet.net/showcase/coffee
```

Actually, all you need to know about using **mosaic** on a very basic level is how to launch it and where to load a Uniform Resource Locator.

You won't end up using most of the command menus, although the **Manuals** and **Help** menus can be helpful when you're looking for further and/or obscure information. Instead, you'll probably use the buttons at the bottom of the **mosaic** window to navigate through the WWW (use the **Back** button to move to previously viewed pages, and so on). And to move between documents, all you do is click on a highlighted hypertext link.

The best way to learn about **mosaic** is to play with it. There's little written documentation for **mosaic**; instead, you can access a ton of **mosaic** information through **mosaic** itself by choosing one of many help resources (found under the **Help** menu) that you download from the NCSA as needed. Using **mosaic** is not an exceptionally difficult task—really, all **mosaic** does is allow you to browse the Web—and after taking a few minutes to run down all your menu choices, you should have a good grasp on the things you can do with **mosaic**.

▼

This Chapter in Review

▲   The Internet was built with UNIX freeware, and the best way to access the vast expanses of the Internet is through UNIX freeware.

▲   Of course, exactly what constitutes Internet access is a matter for you to decide. Access may mean electronic mail, Usenet news, **ftp** and **telnet**, or a direct link to the World Wide Web. The tools in this chapter allow you to accomplish all of them.

▲   Though there are several mail commands that ship with every version of UNIX, freeware offers several better-quality alternatives. One such freeware alternative is Dave Taylor's **elm**, which manages your incoming and outgoing electronic mail.

▲   The **archie** command allows you to search an **archie** server for files that are stored on public FTP sites.

▲   **Gopher** is both a client on your UNIX machine and a database somewhere on the Internet. **Gopher** servers contain vast amounts of information—much of it useful, some of it frivolous.

▲   The World Wide Web, or WWW, is an attempt to create a worldwide hypertext system, where references from one document lead directly to another document. Documents can be WWW sites, **gopher** servers, Usenet newsgroups, or FTP sites.

▲   Several browsers allow you to netsurf the WWW. The most popular UNIX browser is *NCSA Mosaic for the X Window System*.

Little shop of Horrorware

▪ CHAPTER FIVE ▪
Image-Editing Tools

With the emergence of the X Window System as a graphical interface for the UNIX operating system, there's been a corresponding need for graphics utilities that take advantage of this graphical power. The UNIX freeware and shareware community has responded with many useful graphics utilities, including the following, which are covered in this chapter:

- ▲ **Xgrab**, a utility for grabbing screens
- ▲ *Pbmplus*, a set of utilities for converting graphics files
- ▲ Viewing images with **xv**

Working With Graphics Files

As it stands, UNIX doesn't work too well or frequently with graphics formats; after all, UNIX was conceived as a text-only command-line operating system, and in these situations graphics tend to be thrown on as an afterthought. In the case of UNIX, the afterthought was the X Window System, a set of graphical routines written in the C programming language.

Virtually every UNIX systems vendor has adopted the X Window System as the graphical interface of choice, and as a result more and more UNIX users are becoming familiar with the X Window System— or, more than likely, OSF/Motif, a specific look and feel that's built upon the X Window System. As a result, the powerful combination of graphics and UNIX has led to a serious expansion of users' capabilities— powerful image-processing systems based upon UNIX workstations from the likes of Silicon Graphics dominate Hollywood moviemaking, for instance, while the computer-aided design (CAD) and engineering (CAE) worlds are populated by workstations from the likes of Hewlett-Packard and IBM.

With the emergence of graphics as a large reason why people use UNIX, there's been a corresponding need for graphics utilities. This chapter covers the most useful UNIX freeware tools for graphics use, ranging from a simple tool that creates screen dumps to powerful tools for converting and viewing graphics files.

▲ **L E A R N M O R E A B O U T** ▲

Chapter 3 includes some brief coverage of *gnuplot*, an interactive program for plotting mathematical expressions and data distributed by the FSF. It is included on the accompanying CD-ROM.

Except for the *pbmplus* set of utilities, these graphics programs require the X Window System to be running on your system. If you're not sure if you have X Window, check with your system administrator.

Using **Xgrab** and **Xgrabsc**

The X Window System already includes a tool for creating screen dumps: the **xwd** command. So why use a freeware version that also creates screen dumps? Because the **xgrab** screen grabber is both easier to use and more powerful than **xwd**.

If you've used **xwd**, then you know that it's not the best tool for creating screen dumps: It captures an active window or the root window, and the resulting file is in the **xwd** file format, a rather odd little bitmap format that's pretty much useless without some sort of conversion tool (such as *pbmplus*, covered later in this chapter).

By contrast, **xgrab** allows you to capture a screen, a rectangular portion of the screen, a window, or a menu on an immediate or time-delayed basis. It outputs to several formats, but the most useful format will be the Encapsulated PostScript format. Furthermore, it provides a great deal of control over the image itself: You can include the window's borders, dither the image or map it to black and white, reverse the colors, or enhance the brightness.

You can use **xgrabsc** from the UNIX command line housed in an **xterm** window. However, you'll want to use **xgrab**, which is a graphical version of **xgrabsc**. It's disgustingly easy to use, which you'll discover once you launch it with a command line like:

```
$ xgrab
```

Using Pbmplus

Of course, you may want to stick with **xwd**—it does, after all, perform the rudimentary task of creating screen dumps. In this case, however, you'll want to have something that will allow you to actually use these screen dumps; the **xwd** file format is good for displaying screen dumps on the screen (using the **xwud** command) or printing directly to a printer. To actually edit the files or import them into other software, however, you'll need to find a way to convert the **xwd** file to a more useful format.

During the course of writing several books about UNIX and the X Window System, I have found that some UNIX/X Window tools are absolutely essential, especially when working with graphics and the **xwd** file format.

One of those essential utilities is the Portable BitMap Toolkit, known more informally in its most recent release as *pbmplus*. Written by Jef Poskanzer (*jef@well.sf.ca.us*)—who should be a charter member of the UNIX Programmer's Hall of Fame—*pbmplus* allows you to convert files from one graphics format to another.

Pbmplus actually encompasses five parts:

▲ The *pbm* utilities, used for converting bitmaps (1 bit per pixel); they will read only bitmap images

▲ The *pgm* utilities, used for converting grayscale images; they will read both grayscale and bitmap images

▲ The *ppm* utilities, used for converting color images; they will read bitmap, grayscale, and color images

▲ The *pnm* conversion utilities, which works with all formats; this is called the "anymap" format in the *pbmplus* documentation

▲ Various miscellaneous utilities used for editing existing graphics files; for example, the **pnmenlarge** command enlarges any graphics file

Let's run through a typical conversion—one that you might run into, especially if you do any work with the X Window System. After using **xwd** to capture some X Window screens (**xwd**, the X Window Dump utility, is included with the X Window System), you then wonder what to do with the files—the **xwd** file format is somewhat of an odd-ball format, and essentially you can either display an **xwd** file on the screen or print it directly to a printer.

The key to working with *pbmplus* is realizing that any conversion is a two-step process. The first step is to convert to the *ppm* file format, which is a portable bitmap format, and then convert from that format to the destination format. In theory, *pbmplus* works with any graphics file, but the reality is that *pbmplus* works better with bitmap files than vector-based files, in that a bitmap file format defines each bit within an image. A vector format, on the other hands, describes the contents of an image in mathematical terms; while a bitmap format will map out each bit in a line, the vector format will define the line's position within the image and the line's width. This is why there's less support for the Encapsulated PostScript file format, so common in the UNIX world, than you may expect.

With all of this in mind, you're ready to convert the file. Your first step will be to convert from the **xwd** format to the **ppm** or **pnm** formats. Converting to the **ppm** or **pnm** formats is usually your first course of action, as these formats act as bridges between formats—there's very little direct conversion between formats within *pbmplus*. If your original screen **xwd** dump is named **dump.xwd**, you'd use the following command line to convert the file:

```
$ xwdtopnm dump.xwd > dump.pnm
```

As you know, UNIX doesn't require the use of three-character suffixes to filenames. However, when you're working with graphics files and converting between different file formats, it's a good idea to tag on a suffix that describes the file format—suffixes like *.xwd* allow you to keep track of the different files. In addition, the PC world makes heavy use of suffixes like *.pcx* in its graphics utilities; often the only way to tell the format of a file is through its descriptive suffix.

In this step, you've converted the **xwd** file to the **ppm** format—the bridge format between other formats.

Remember, there's no such format as the **pnm** format. Instead, when you invoke a *pbmplus* command that includes **pnm**, you're really telling **pbmplus** to use the highest-level file format available.

The second step will be to convert the **pnm** format to your destination format. Since the **pcx** file format is popular on many computer platforms, you may want to convert to this format using the following command line:

```
$ ppmtopcx dump.pnm > dump.pcx
```

You can use the resulting file in any application that supports the **pcx** file format, including any graphics utility that runs under Microsoft *Windows*.

Why **ppm** and not **pnm**? If you look for a filename like **pnmtopcx**, you're not going to find it. On the other hand, you will find the filename **ppmtopcx**. Remember, the **pbm**-type command can be used with almost any file format, also.

This is technical

This leads to one of the problems with *pbmplus*: It can be rather confusing for new UNIX users to use. Doing a list of filenames in the directory storing **pbmplus** executables yields a *long* list of files, such as:

```
anytopnm
fstopgm
pbmtomac
pnmtops
pnmtorast
pnmtotiff
rasttopnm
tifftopnm
xwdtopbm
xwdtopnm
```

Your best bet is to go through the file of filenames and match your original or intended format with the highest-level **pnm** format. Since the **pnm** format is the universal format, you'll want to check for a filename like:

yourformattopnm

In the case of the example outlined earlier, there was indeed such a file that could be used on the original image: **xwdtopnm**. However, when looking for something to convert the **pnm** file to the **pcx** format, it's pretty clear that the **pbmtopcx** command will have to do. The advice is to use commands that begin with *ppm* and *pnm* as often as possible. (As the documentation states: "Don't even try to remember what's what.")

There is one saving grace for the neophyte UNIX user, however: The documentation for *pbmplus*, while concise, is actually pretty useful. And there's the added advantage of having each command self-contained within a file—you can list the contents of a directory and narrow the search down for all filenames ending in *pcx* or your favorite file format.

In Tables 5.1, 5.2, 5.3, and 5.4, the names of file formats are listed by the type of image (black and white, gray, or color). Included within the format listed is an italicized portion of the filename(s) associated with the file format; for instance, the *pcx* listed next to the PC Paintbrush file format can be combined with the **ls** command to find a file named **ppmtopcx**, which will convert between the **pbm** file format and the **pcx** file format.

TABLE 5.1   BLACK-AND-WHITE IMAGE FORMATS SUPPORTED BY PBM

FORMAT	READING	WRITING
Sun icon file (*icon*)	x	x
X10 bitmap file (*x10bm*)	x	x
X11 bitmap file (*xbm*)	x	x
MacPaint (*macp*)	x	x
CMU window-manager format (*cmuwm*)	x	x
MGR format (*mgr*)	x	x

TABLE 5.1 CONTINUED

FORMAT	READING	WRITING
Group 3 FAX (*g3*)	x	x
GEM .IMG format (*gem*)	x	x
Bennet Yee's "face" format (*ybm*)	x	x
Atari Degas .PI3 format (*pi3*)	x	x
Andrew Toolkit raster object (*atk*)	x	x
Xerox doodle brushes (*brush*)	x	
ASCII graphics (*ascii*)		x
HP LaserJet format (*lj*)		x
GraphOn graphics (*go*)		x
BBN BitGraphgraphics (*bbnbg*)		x
Printronix format (*ptx*)		x
Gemini 10x printer format (*10x*)		x
Epson printer format (*epson*)		x
UNIX plot(5) file (*plot*)		x
Zinc Interface		x
Library icon (*zinc*)		x

TABLE 5.2 GREYSCALE IMAGE FORMATS SUPPORTED BY PGM

FORMAT	READING	WRITING
PostScript "image" data (*psid*)	x	
Usenix FaceSaver File (*fs*)	x	x
FITS (*fits*)	x	x
Lisp Machine bit-array-file (*lispm*)	x	x
Raw grayscale bytes (*raw*)	x	
HIPS (*hips*)	x	

TABLE 5.3 COLOR IMAGE FORMATS SUPPORTED BY PPM

FORMAT	READING	WRITING
GIF (*gif*)	X	X
IFF ILBM (*ilbm*)	X	X
Macintosh PICT (*pict*)	X	X
Atari Degas .pi1 format (*pi1*)	X	X
XPM (X Window pixmaps) (*xpm*)	X	X
PC Paintbrush PCX format (*pcx*)	X	X
TrueVision Targa file (*tga*)	X	X
HP PaintJet format (*pj*)	X	X
Abekas YUV format (*yuv*)	X	X
MTV/PRT ray-tracer output (*mtv*)	X	
Gould scanner file (*gould*)	X	
QRT ray-tracer output (*qrt*)	X	
Img-whatnot file (*img*)	X	
Xim file (*xim*)	X	
Atari uncompressed Spectrum (*spu*)	X	
Atari compressed Spectrum (*spc*)	X	
NCSA Interactive Color Raster (*rast*)	X	
X11 "puzzle" file (*puzz*)	X	
Motif UIL icon file (*uil*)	X	
DEC sixel format (*sixel*)	X	
AutoCAD slide format (*sld*)	X	X
AutoCAD DXB format (*dxb*)		X

TABLE 5.4 MULTITYPE IMAGE FORMATS SUPPORTED BY PNM

FORMAT	READING	WRITING
Sun raster file (*rast*)	X	X
TIFF (*tif*)	X	X
X11 window dump file (*xwd*)	X	X
X10 window dump file (*xwd*)	X	X
PostScript (*ps*)		X

Viewing Images with Xv

After you've converted files to and fro, you can use **xv** to view them.

An essential utility for any X Window user, **xv** allows you to view and edit image files. Developed by John Bradley (*bradley@cis.upenn.edu*) at the University of Pennsylvania, **Xv** supports the following file formats:

▲ GIF

▲ JPEG

▲ TIFF

▲ PBM

▲ PGM

▲ PPM

▲ X11 bitmap

▲ Utah Raster Tookit RLE

▲ PDS/VICAR

▲ Sun raster file

▲ BMP

▲ PCX

▲ IRIS RGB

▲ PostScript

▲ PM

You can run **xv** from the command line, either with a graphics file loaded:

$ xv graphic.tiff

or without a graphics file loaded:

$ xv

In addition, there are a number of handy command-line options for **xv**. Some of the more useful options are listed in Table 5.5.

TABLE 5.5 USEFUL COMMAND-LINE OPTIONS FOR THE XV COMMAND

OPTION	RESULT
-geometry	Sets the window geometry.
-help	Displays instructions for using **xv**, as well as a complete set of command-line options.
-max	Displays the image across the full screen, even if the image must be distorted to do so.
-root	Displays the image in the root window, which means the image will always be in the background.

Using Xv

With **xv** loaded, take a few minutes to play with the menus. There's nothing too complicated with **xv** when it comes to displaying screen images.

However, don't forget that **xv** can also be used to edit screen images, too. For instance, you may want to use **xv** to crop your ex-spouse out of a portrait you've stored in a JPEG file. In this case, you'll want to select the rectangular part of the JPEG image you want to retain. Do this by pressing the middle mouse button at the corner of the rectangular portion, and then keep the button pressed down while you drag the rectangular portion across the screen. You can create rectangles as many times as you want; there's nothing permanent about any rectangle, so if you don't like what you've done, you can just start again.

Once you're decided on the part of the image you want to retain, press the **c** (for *crop*) key, and the portion of the image outside the rectangle will disappear. If you decide that you want to retain your ex-spouse in the picture, press **u** (for *uncrop*).

This Chapter in Review

▲ With an emerging emphasis on graphics, UNIX now features a set of useful graphics utilities.

▲ **Xgrabsc** and **xgrab** are used to grab screen images. Because of their additional capabilities, they outdo the **xwd** utility that's included with almost every implementation of the X Window System.

▲ The *pbmplus* series of utilities convert graphics files between a huge set of possible formats, including some obscure formats and many frequently used formats in the UNIX, DOS, *Windows*, and Macintosh environments.

▲   The **xv** utility displays images either within a window or
as the root window. It supports a wide range of formats,
including the proprietary formats generated by *pbmplus*,
the X bitmap format, and mainstream formats like PC
Paintbrush and PostScript.

▪ CHAPTER SIX ▪
Games

All work and no play leaves you a tired and bored computer user. That's why some neat games are included within this book, including:

▲ **Xtetris**, an X Window version of the popular game

▲ **Gnuchess**, a chess game

▲ **Nethack**, a D&D game

▲ Miscellaneous games line **xmahjonng** and **xsol**

Fooling Around With Your System

Games have a rich and proud tradition within the UNIX operating system. A glance at UNIX history shows that games—and, specifically, the game *Space Travel*—were part of the UNIX operating system from the very beginning.

Sure, games can eat up precious resources (especially any game written under the X Window System), and games can certainly eat up a lot of your time (don't tell your bosses that you're using this book to install games when you ask for reimbursement), but games are an integral part of any computer user's education. Really.

Xtetris

Perhaps one of the most addicting computer games ever created was *Tetris*, ostensibly created by a set of Russian programmers. In a more paranoid age, the emergence of *Tetris* would have been seen by conspiracists as a Russian plan to tie up untold computing cycles while the evil Russkies were planning to take over the world. Now, in this enlightened post-Cold War age, we can merely view *Tetris* as a healthy diversion for fun-loving Westerners.

The goal of *Tetris* is simple. As blocks of various sizes and shapes fall from the sky, your job is to rotate and move the blocks so that they fall in an orderly manner, eliminating any gaps between blocks. If you create an entire row of blocks without a gap, the row then disappears, the computer voices its approval in the form of a beep, and your score rises. If you allow a gap in a row, that row stays on the screen, with subsequent blocks covering it. As the rows rise, you have less time to react to new blocks falling from the sky. When the pile of blocks reaches the top of the *Tetris* window, the game is over. Your score is then compared to the high scores contained in a separate file, and if you've made the top ten, you're inducted into the *Tetris* hall of fame.

How do you score points? Obviously, by eliminating rows of blocks. But *Tetris* also gives you some credit for style. If you've got a block in perfect position near the top of the screen, you can drop it early by pressing either the middle mouse button or the space bar. The higher the block, the more points you'll receive.

The *Tetris* version on the accompanying CD-ROM is **xtetris**, written for the X Window System. To use it, you'll need Release 5 of the X Window System (unfortunately, it will not compile under Release 4), according to the authors. Launching **xtetris** is simple: You merely use the following command line:

```
$ xtetris
```

There are a few command-line options for **xtetris**, as listed in Table 6.1.

TABLE 6.I SOME COMMAND-LINE OPTIONS FOR XTETRIS

OPTION	RESULT
-bw	Runs the game in black and white. (If you're running this game on a black-and-white system, you'll want to explicitly set this option.)
-color	Runs the game in color (this is the default).
-noscore	Does not access the file containing high scores when playing **xtetris**.
-score	Uses the **scorefile** when playing **xtetris** (this is the default).

You can play **xtetris** with the mouse, the keyboard, or cursor keys. Commands for all three methods are listed in Tables 6.2, 6.3, and 6.4.

TABLE 6.2 MOUSE COMMANDS FOR XTETRIS

PRESSING...	RESULTS IN...
Left mouse button	The block moving to the left.
Right mouse button	The block moving to the right.
Middle mouse button	The block falling to the bottom.
Shift-left mouse button	The block rotating counterclockwise.
Shift-right mouse button	The block rotating clockwise.

TABLE 6.3 KEYBOARD COMMANDS FOR XTETRIS

PRESSING...	RESULTS IN...
h	The block moving to the left.
l	The block moving to the right (this is pretty counterintuitive, if you stop to think about it).
Space bar	The block falling to the bottom.
j	The block rotating clockwise.
k	The block rotating counterclockwise.

TABLE 6.4 CURSOR-KEY MOVEMENTS FOR XTETRIS

PRESSING...	RESULTS IN...
←	The block moving to the left.
→	The block moving to the right.
↓	The block rotating clockwise.
↑	The block rotating counterclockwise.
Space bar	The block falling to the bottom.

Playing Gnuchess

The **gnuchess** game was covered briefly in Chapter 3. However, it's worth another mention here, as it's one of the better computer-based chess games available—and unless you watch yourself, **gnuchess** is capable of beating you. Originally, **gnuchess** was a rather rudimentary chess game—the author, Stuart Cracraft (*cracraft@wheaties.ai.mit.edu*) characterized it as a Class D player—but since that time it has been improved to where it can be regarded as a Master player.

If you are a serious chess player, you'll want to check through the **gnuchess** documentation, which outlines the strategies—essentially, the Shannon Type-A and Type-B method—incorporated into the game.

There are several ways to play **gnuchess**, depending on what command line you use to launch the program. The differences lie in how the game is presented on your screen; you don't need the X Window System to run **gnuchess**, although there is an option for running **gnuchess** under X. The methods are listed in Table 6.5.

TABLE 6.5 VARIOUS PERMUTATIONS OF GNUCHESS

COMMAND LINE	RESULT
gnuchess	Curses-based chess game.
gnuchessc	Chesstool-compatible chess game.
gnuchessn	Curses-based chess game with a flashier interface.
gnuchessr	ASCII-based chess game.
gnuchessx	X Window-based chess game.

There's one other option for **gnuchess**: a timer. By passing a numeral as part of the command line, you can specify the time the game has to complete a move. A command line of:

```
$ gnuchess 25
```

would set a time of 25 seconds. A command line of:

```
$ gnuchess 3:15
```

would set a time of 3 minutes, 15 seconds.

You can also set a time limit in combination with a precise number of moves. (Experienced chess players will recognize this as a must for any serious chess competition.) For example, you may want to tell **gnuchess** to perform 100 moves in 10 minutes. By using a command line with two numerical arguments, as in the following, you can do just that:

```
$ gnuchess 100 10
```

▼

The previous time specifications can be applied to all of the **gnuchess** variations listed in Table 6.5.

Specifying Your Moves

Unfortunately, **gnuchess** isn't the most graphical of applications. In many situations, you'll use the keyboard to specify your moves. **Gnuchess** responds to the traditional chess-based board notation, which combines the name of the piece (*p* for pawn, *b* for bishop, *r* for rook, *q* for queen, *k* for king, and *n* for knight) and the coordinates of the board (B-4, E-5, etc.). Other more complicated moves, such as castling, are explained in the documentation.

> ### ▲ L E A R N   M O R E   A B O U T ▲
>
> Two other GNU games are included on the accompanying CD-ROM; these games were covered briefly in Chapter 3. **Gnugo** is a computer-based version of the Go game, while **acm** is a networked X Window air-combat game.

Nethack: A Computer-Based Dungeons and Dragons

Hardcore computer users seem to have a fascination with Dungeons and Dragons, whether it be playing the board game in a basement or playing a computer-based version in their corporate cubicle.

The **nethack** game has a long and storied history in the UNIX world, so its inclusion on the accompanying CD-ROM shouldn't be a surprise for any experienced UNIX user. The goal in **nethack** is simple: recover the Amulet of Yendor, located deep within a dungeon. Along the way, you earn points for said recovery; in addition, you can also amass points for bringing back gold to the surface after recovering the Amulet.

Be warned that **nethack** isn't the easiest game to master. Like other Dungeons and Dragons progeny, there's a steep learning curve before you even begin to realize exactly how the game is structured. There's an additional learning period devoted to mastering the incredibly dense user interface.

A ton of information is displayed on the screen, but what it exactly means isn't apparent without some heavy-duty consultation with the documentation; for instance, the usage of % as portraying food isn't the most intuitive of designs.

And the language used to communicate with the game, while an improvement on previous **nethack** versions, still is fairly obtuse— especially for a beginner.

The bottom line: **Nethack** can be a hoot to play. But be prepared to spend the time necessary to master it (which includes a ton of time spent burrowing within the documentation), and don't be frustrated when your initial efforts lead you to early failures.

Additional Games

Also included on the CD-ROM are some additional games that you might find useful. For the Mah-jongg players out there, there's a pretty good version for X Window System users called **xmahjongg**. For Solitaire players, there's **xsol**, which sticks to the Vegas rules of Solitaire.

This Chapter in Review

▲ Games are why we use computers. Forget about database applications, spreadsheets, or CAD/CAM—admit it, games rule.

▲ **Xtetris** is an X Window version of the popular *Tetris* game. Your goal is to make sure that falling blocks are aligned properly—a task that most fastidious computer users will find to be extremely challenging and rewarding.

▲ **Gnuchess** is the GNU version of chess. It has been improved over the years and should prove to be quite a challenge.

▲ **Nethack** is a venerable UNIX Dungeons and Dragons-type game. In it, your goal is to descend into the bowels of the earth and retrieve an amulet, as well as plundering the underworld of its gold. Go to town, kids.

▪ CHAPTER SEVEN ▪
Communications Tools

Even though networking and communications are built into the UNIX operating system, there are ways to enhance these capabilities through freeware and shareware. Tools covered in this chapter include:

▲ **Pcomm**, a UNIX shareware version of the popular DOS *Procomm* program

▲ The **kermit** telecommunications package

▲ **Rz** and **sz**, which allow you to send and receive files using the Zmodem protocol

Using Pcomm for Communications

UNIX has a big advantage over other operating systems—communications and networking are both built within the base operating system.

But these communications capabilities can be a little on the obtuse side (something you know if you've perused another book in the UNIX Fundamentals series, *UNIX Communications and Networking*), especially commands like **cu**, used to communicate directly with online systems.

▲ **L E A R N   M O R E   A B O U T** ▲

Chapter 3 covers some additional programs that are useful when working with communications, including *gzip*.

The solution can be found in the UNIX freeware world in the form of **pcomm**, a communications utility patterned after Datastorm Technologies' popular DOS-based *Procomm Plus* telecommunications program. The original shareware version of *Procomm Plus* was a menu-based program; you entered the names, phone numbers, and communications parameters for any number of online systems, and *Procomm Plus* did the rest.

The same is true of **pcomm**. You can create entries for various online services and bulletin-board services. If you want to transfer files, you can use one of the following protocols:

- ▲ xmodem
- ▲ xmodem-1k
- ▲ modem7
- ▲ ymodem
- ▲ ymodem-g
- ▲ ASCII
- ▲ zmodem

You can also add your own protocol, although reality dictates that your only serious choice in this matter is **kermit** (which is also included on the accompanying CD-ROM). In most circumstances, the previous list of protocols will suffice.

If you're unfamiliar with these protocols, here's a hint: Generally speaking, you'll get the best performance with zmodem, although some **kermit** purists argue that **kermit** performance can be equal to zmodem performance.

Starting **pcomm** is a matter of the following command line:

```
$ pcomm
```

Pcomm then takes over the screen and displays a status line that gives you the name of the TTY device in use, the line setting, the data-logging and printing-logging status, and the key summoning help. This status line is always present.

Pcomm Commands

Pcomm is a command-driven environment once you get past the dialing directory. To send **pcomm** a command, you need to get its attention by first typing **Ctrl-a**, following by one of the many commands listed in Table 7.1. For the most part, these are the same commands that are supported by the DOS-based *Procomm* program.

TABLE 7.1 FREQUENTLY USED PCOMM COMMANDS

COMMAND	RESULT
PageUp	Sets the file-transfer protocol used to upload files to the online service.
PageDn	Sets the file-transfer protocol used to download files from the online service.

TABLE 7.I CONTINUED

COMMAND	RESULT
0 (zero)	Displays a help screen.
1 (one)	Opens a log of the current session; will prompt for a filename.
B	Changes the current working directory; file transfers are automatically sent to or pulled from the current working directory.
C	Clears the screen.
D	Summons the dialing directory.
G	Stores the current screen to a file.
H	Hangs up the phone connection.
M	Displays a menu that allows you to manually dial a telephone number.
L	Prints dialing directory to either a specified file or the printer.
P	Changes the current communications parameters.
R	Redials the selected dialing-directory entry.
S	Displays setup screens.
X	Exits **pcomm**.

Customizing Pcomm

One of the advantages of *Procomm* is its powerful scripting language. While **pcomm** doesn't feature the same scripting language, it does allow you to call UNIX shell scripts once you're connected to an online system. These scripts can be used for something as mundane as actually logging in a remote system, or something as complicated as grabbing new messages from a discussion on a bulletin-board system. In addition, **pcomm** features several programs that can be summoned within a script, all relating to telecommunications-specific functions. In these situations, you'll want to refer to the documentation for more information.

A Matter of Protocols: Kermit and Zmodem

A file-transfer protocol manages the transfer of files between system that are connected over a modem and telephone lines. As you saw in the previous discussion of **pcomm**, there are a number of protocols in use in the computer world. Though there's some debate when comparing performance, two of the most popular protocols are **kermit** and **zmodem**.

Both protocols are contained on the accompanying CD-ROM, albeit in slightly different formats. The venerable **kermit** program is a complete telecommunications program, allowing you to specify the parameters of a communications session with another remote system. This includes the telephone number of the remote system, the communications settings (bits-per-second rate, etc.), modem type (in this date and age, usually the ubiquitous Hayes format), and so on. However, the remote system must also be running **kermit** in some form, which limits its utility. (Many older mainframe systems, particularly in academic settings, still make use of **kermit**, however.)

Be warned that the documentation for **kermit** is rather on the obtuse side. It's not the easiest package to install and use.

By contrast, support for the Zmodem protocol is accomplished with two commands: **sz** (used to send files with the zmodem protocol) and **rz** (used to receive files with the zmodem protocol). (On the accompanying CD-ROM the program name begins with *rzsz*, not *zmodem*.)

The **sz** and **rz** commands are used once there's already a connection with a remote system. (The UNIX **cu** command will do just that.) As a protocol, zmodem is *the* protocol of a choice in high-performance situations, as throughput is substantially better than other older protocols like xmodem and ymodem (though there are some **kermit** fans who argue otherwise).

The nice thing about the zmodem protocol is that much of the transfer is automated. You don't need to receive the specific name of a file before downloading it from a remote system; that information is sent at the beginning of a zmodem session.

To send a file named *chapter7*, you'd use a command line like the following:

```
$ sz chapter7
```

This command line assumes that the defaults for **sz** are adequate—and for the most part, they will be. However, if you do need to change these defaults, you'll do so on the command line, through a series of options, as listed in Table 7.2.

TABLE 7.2 COMMAND-LINE OPTIONS FOR THE SZ COMMAND

OPTION	RESULT
+	Appends incoming data to an existing file.
-a	Converts newline characters to CR/LF (carriage return/line feed). This option is important when sending files for usage on DOS or Macintosh systems.
-b	Sends files with no binary translations.
-k	Sends files in larger blocks (1,024-byte blocks, as opposed to the default 128-byte blocks).

TABLE 7.4 CONTINUED

OPTION	RESULT
-n	Sends a file if the file doesn't exist on the remote system; if it does, then *sz* will overwrite the destination file if it's older than the file to be send.
-p	Refuses to send to the file if it exists on the remote system.
-y	Overwrites existing file on remote system.

The same process is true for receiving files from the remote system: Simply begin a zmodem file transfer on the remote system, and then invoke **rz**:

```
$ rz
```

Again, the defaults for **rz** should suffice. If they don't, you can select from one of the command-line options listed in Table 7.3.

TABLE 7.3 COMMAND-LINE OPTIONS FOR THE RZ COMMAND

OPTION	RESULT
-a	Strips carriage returns from the file to meet UNIX conventions.
-p	File is not transferred if it already exists on your system.
-y	Overwrites existing files on your system.

This Chapter in Review

▲ Even though communications is built directly into the UNIX operating system, there are some UNIX freeware and shareware tools you can use to enhance these capabilities.

▲ For most users, the **pcomm** telecommunications program will be easier to use than the standard UNIX communications commands. Based upon the DOS *Procomm* telecommunications shareware, **pcomm** is menu-driven software that allows you to choose from a large dialing directory and to connect directly to remote systems.

▲ The **kermit** program also allows you to connect to remote systems. However, **kermit** is more difficult to use than **pcomm**.

▲ Once connected, you can speed up file transfers by using the **rz** and **sz** commands. These commands send and receive files using the speedy zmodem file-transfer protocol.

▪ CHAPTER EIGHT ▪
Miscellaneous UNIX and X Tools

Not every UNIX freeware and shareware program fits into the nice product categories found in the previous chapters. This chapter covers some of these other programs, including:

- ▲ **Screen**, which allows you to use multiple screens on a dumb terminal
- ▲ **Calc tool**, a replacement calculator
- ▲ A couple of clocks
- ▲ **Less**, a substitute for the **more** and **page** commands

Ever Such a Lot of Odds and Sods

Given the history of the UNIX operating system, it's no surprise that there's a lot of UNIX freeware and shareware that transcends classification. Some of these freeware titles are for fun only, while other tools can be truly useful, depending on your needs.

This chapter covers various miscellaneous UNIX freeware and shareware tools. You probably won't find all of these tools to be useful or even applicable, but take a browse through these listings—you just never know. (On the other hand, anyone using a plain text terminal will appreciate the power of the first freeware covered in this chapter, **screen**.)

Using Screen to Manage Multiple Screens

One of the big advantages of working with the X Window System is its ability to manage multiple windows. You can be running a word processor in one screen, an **xterm** and a UNIX command line in another, and an Internet **mosaic** session in yet another. Moving between them is a breeze; just click your mouse over the window you want to activate.

These advantages aren't available to anyone not running the X Window System, however, unless you use a neat utility called **screen**. The **screen** utility allows you to run multiple sessions on your screen; you can move between full-screen sessions (which, confusingly enough, are called *windows*—but not windows in the sense of the X Window System), scroll back through the previous contents of a window, and cut-and-paste data between sessions.

This is technical

There's an older **screen** utility that serves as the basis of the current **screen** utility. To eliminate confusion, the new version is really called **iscreen**. However, the documentation still refers to the utility as **screen**, and it's known by that name, so that's what will be used in this book.

Launching **screen** is a matter of a command line like the following:

$ screen

Screen also features a number of command-line options, some of which are listed in Table 8.1.

TABLE 8.1 COMMAND-LINE OPTIONS FOR THE SCREEN COMMAND

COMMAND	RESULT
-a	Summons all possible command-line options.
-A	Adjusts the size of the windows to the size of the display.
-h num	Sets the history scrollback buffer to be *num* lines.

This is technical

Screen will not run on a UNIX system that doesn't feature UNIX domain sockets, the *select* system call, or psuedo-ttys.

After you've launched **screen**, you're presented with a shell prompt, from which you can perform your normal computing tasks, such as running applications or entering UNIX commands at the shell prompt. (It may not appear that anything is different, past the clearing of the screen.) However, you can now send any number of commands to **screen**, telling it to create new windows. Once you've got a number of screens created, you can also switch between screens in a variety of ways.

To send a command to **screen**, you first need to get its attention by typing **Ctrl-a**; after that, you enter one-letter commands, as listed in Table 8.2.

This is technical

There are times when you might run into problems when entering commands via the **Ctrl-a** method. These situations occur when an application assumes that the **Ctrl-a** is meant for it and not the **screen** program. In these cases, you'll need to make some changes in the program's configuration file, **.screenrc**, as detailed in the documentation.

TABLE 8.2 SOME FREQUENTLY USED COMMANDS FOR SCREEN

COMMAND	RESULT
Ctrl-a	Switches to the previous window.
Ctrl-	Kills all windows and then ends **screen**.
Space bar	Switches to the next window.
?	Summons a help screen.
num	Switches to the window numbered *num*.
c	Creates a new window and makes that new window the current window
C	Clears the screen.
h	Prints the current window to the **hardcopy.n** file.
k	Closes the current windows and switches to the previous window.
p	Switches to the previous window.

Note this

There are a few points to be reviewed from Table 8.2. Yes, it is true that you'll need to use a **Ctrl-a Ctrl-a** combination to switch to the previous windows. With these commands, case indeed does count, so be careful not to use **C** when you really want to use **c**.

Don't be surprised if **screen** doesn't work perfectly right out of the chute. This program relies on some tricks to do its magic, and those tricks require a little configuration work on your end before everything falls together. The documentation is pretty good about what needs to be done to make **screen** work.

Calctool

UNIX users love their calculators. On the accompanying CD-ROM is **calctool**, a hexadecimal calculator. It's more sophisticated than the standard calculators shipped with the X Window System, and also easier to use than the calculators shipped by other UNIX vendors.

What Time Is It?

UNIX and X Window users are definitely Type A creatures; they love to have a clock right on the screen at times. The X Window System ships with a decent-looking clock; however, that hasn't stopped some enterprising programmers from creating their own.

The **swisswatch** clock includes emulation of the commonly found **oclock**, as well as a Swiss railway-clock emulation and a snazzy default appearance.

Xc_clock runs on Linux and SCO OpenDesktop systems and is an interactive clock, which means you can change the time displayed on the clock at whim.

Using Less, Not More

UNIX hacks certainly don't lack a punning sense of humor: witness the moniker for the **less** utility, which can be viewed as a replacement for the **more** command.

The less utility was designed as an improvement to the **more** and **page** commands, allowing you more control (so to speak) over the display of a document.

Less scrolls a document.

To use **less**, specify it on a command line, with the name of a file to view:

```
$ less textfile
```

You're not limited to a single file; you could view multiple files consecutively, as in the following command line:

```
$ less textfile1 testfile2 textfile3
```

> ### ▲ L E A R N   M O R E   A B O U T ▲
>
> There are several command-line options to **less**, which will be covered later in this chapter.

Moving through the document can be quite easy if you're used to working with the text editor **vi**.

> ### ▲ L E A R N   M O R E   A B O U T ▲
>
> Remember, you learned about **vi** in Chapter 2.

If you're not used to working with the **vi** editor, you may be in for a few surprises.

Keep in mind at all times that you're scrolling through a document. You're not editing the document. Therefore, you can do *anything* and not harm the document in any way.

Indeed, the most confusing thing about **less** is that it gives you a ton of different ways to perform the same task (perhaps under the assumption that, like the proverbial blind pig running across the proverbial acorn, you'll somehow stumble across the correct command). To move forward a specified number of lines, you could use any of the following commands:

▲ e

▲ **Ctrl-E**

▲ **j**

▲ **Ctrl-N**

▲ **Return** key

In addition, you could combine these commands with a numeral to specify the number of lines you want to move forward. For instance, if you typed **21**, followed by the **Return** key, you'd move the document forward by 21 lines.

A summary of commands from the **less** documentation is listed in Table 8.3.

TABLE 8.3 SOME COMMANDS FOR THE LESS PROGRAM

COMMAND	RESULT
h H	Displays a help screen.
q :q :Q ZZ	Exits **less**.
F	Forwards the document forever; like **tail -f**.
r Ctrl-R Ctrl-L	Repaints the screen.
R	Repaint screen, discarding buffered input.
m *letter*	Marks the current position with *letter*.
'*letter*	Goes to a previously marked position.

TABLE 8.3 CONTINUED

COMMAND	RESULT
h H	Displays a help screen.
q :q :Q ZZ	Exits **less**.
F	Forwards the document forever; like **tail -f**.
r Ctrl-R Ctrl-L	Repaints the screen.
R	Repaint screen, discarding buffered input.
m *letter*	Marks the current position with *letter*.
'*letter*	Goes to a previously marked position.
" *or* **Ctrl-XCtrl-X**	Goes to the previous position.
E *filename*	Examines a new file.
:e Ctrl-XCtrl-V	Examines a new file.
= Ctrl-G :f	Prints current file name.
-*flag*	Toggles a command-line *flag*.
_*flag*	Displays the settings of a command-line *flag*.
+cmd	Executes the **less** command each time a new file is examined.
!*command*	Passes the *command* to $SHELL to be executed.
\X*command*	Pipes file between current position and marks *X* to shell command.
v	Edit the current file with $EDITOR.

TABLE 8.3 CONTINUED

COMMAND   RESULT

These commands moves a document one line or screen at a time if there's no numeral given; if a numeral is given, the document is moved that many screens or lines.

COMMAND	MOVES DOCUMENT....
e Ctrl-E j Ctrl-N Return	Forward one line.
y Ctrl-Y k Ctrl-K Ctrl-P	Backward one line.
f Ctrl-F Ctrl-V space bar	Forward one window.
b Ctrl-B Esc-v	Backward one window.
z	Forward one window.
w	Backward one window.
d Ctrl-D	Forward one half-window.
u Ctrl-U	Backward one half-window.
g	To first line in file.
G	To last line in file.
p %	To beginning of file (or a percentage into the file, if a numeral is given)

These searching commands can also be used in conjunction with a number; to precede these commands with a number, such as 5, would tell the command to search for the fifth instance of the *pattern*.

COMMAND	RESULT
/pattern	Searches forward for matching line.
?pattern	Searches backward for matching line.

Search commands may be modified by one or more of:

! search for NON-matching lines

* search multiple files

@ start search at first file (for /) or last file (for ?).

TABLE 8.3 CONTINUED

COMMAND	RESULT
n	Repeats previous search (for occurrence).
N	Repeat previous search in reverse direction.
Esc-n	Repeats previous search, spanning files.
Esc-N	Repeats previous search, reverse directory and spanning files.

Changing Settings on the Fly

A nice thing about **less** is that you can change the command-line options on the fly. (You can also set these options on the command line, of course.) For example, you could change the size of the screen or the way the file scrolls across the screen in the middle of a session, rather than by stating **less** from scratch.

The command-line options are shown in Table 8.4.

TABLE 8.4 COMMAND-LINE OPTIONS FOR THE LESS COMMAND

These flags may be changed either on the command line, or from within less by using the - command.

FLAG	RESULT
-?	Display help (from command line).
-a	Sets forward search starting location.
-b *num*	Sets *num* of buffers.
-B	Automatically allocates buffers.

TABLE 8.4 CONTINUED

These flags may be changed either on the command line, or from within less by using the - command.

FLAG	RESULT
-c -C	Repaints the screen by scrolling/clearing.
-?	Display help (from command line).
-a	Sets forward search starting location.
-b *num*	Sets *num* of buffers.
-B	Automatically allocates buffers.
-c -C	Repaints the screen by scrolling/clearing.
-d	Sets up a dumb terminal.
-e -E	Quits at end of file.
-f	Forces open nonregular files.
-h *num*	Sets backward scroll limit as *num*.
-I	Ignores case in searches.
-j *num*	Sets screen position of target lines as *num*.
-k *file*	Uses a lesskey *file*.
-m -M	Sets a prompt style.
-n -N	Uses line numbers.
-o *file*	Sets a log *file*.
-O *file*	Sets a log *file* (unconditionally overwrite).
-p *pattern*	Starts at *pattern* (from command line).
-P *prompt*	Defines a new prompt.
-q -Q	Quiets the terminal bell.
-r	Translates control characters.
-s	Squeezes multiple blank lines.
-S	Chops long lines.
-t *tag*	Finds a *tag*.
-T *tagfile*	Uses an alternate *tagfile*.

TABLE 8.4 CONTINUED

FLAG	RESULT
-u -U	Changes handling of backspaces.
-w	Displays ~ (tilde character) for lines after end-of-file.
-x *num*	Sets tab stops.
-y *num*	Sets the forward scroll limit.
-z *num*	Sets the size of window.

Customize to Your Heart's Content

If you don't like the way **less** does something, you're perfectly free to change it. For example, you may want to change the key bindings used to summon any of the commands.

Doing so is a somewhat involved, though not very complex, sequence. In essence, you'll be setting up your own file (**.less**) of key bindings, and then running the **lesskey** command to incorporate your changes into the file that stores the key bindings. **Less** uses a stylized method of notating commands, as you can see in Table 8.5: By combining a key with **forw-line**, you'd be telling **less** that you want your specified, new key to move the document forward by a line. For example, your **.less** file should contain the following line to tie the = key to **forw-line**:

```
= forw-line
```

After installing **less**, check the **man** pages (explained in the appendix) for the specific details on changing these keys.

TABLE 8.5 UTILITY ACTIONS FOR THE LESS COMMAND

KEY	ACTION
j	forw-line
Ctrl-E	forw-line
Ctrl-N	forw-line
k	back-line
y	back-line
Ctrl-Y	back-line
Ctrl-K	back-line
Ctrl-P	back-line
J	forw-line-force
K	back-line-force
Y	back-line-force
d	forw-scroll
Ctrl-D	forw-scroll
u	back-scroll
Ctrl-U	back-scroll
'	back-scroll
\40	forw-screen
f	forw-screen
Ctrl-F	forw-screen
Ctrl-V	forw-screen
b	back-screen
Ctrl-B	back-screen
\33v	back-screen
z	forw-window
w	back-window
F	forw-forever
R	repaint-flush

TABLE 8.5 CONTINUED

KEY	ACTION
r	repaint
Ctrl-R	repaint
Ctrl-L	repaint
g	goto-line
<	goto-line
\33<	goto-line
p	percent
%	percent
{	forw-bracket {}
}	back-bracket {}
(	forw-bracket ()
)	back-bracket ()
[	forw-bracket []
]	back-bracket []
\33Ctrl-F	forw-bracket
\33Ctrl-B	back-bracket
G	goto-end
\33>	goto-end
>	goto-end
P	goto-end
=	status
Ctrl-G	status
:f	status
/	forw-search
?	back-search
\33/	forw-search
\33?	back-search

TABLE 8.5 CONTINUED

n	repeat-search
\33n	repeat-search-all
N	reverse-search
\33N	reverse-search-all
m	set-mark
'	goto-mark
Ctrl-XCtrl-X	goto-mark
E	examine
:e	examine
Ctrl-XCtrl-V	examine
:n	next-file
:p	prev-file
:x	index-file
-	toggle-option
:t	toggle-option t
s	toggle-option o
_	display-option
|	pipe
v	visual
!	shell
+	firstcmd
H	help
h	help
V	version
q	quit
:q	quit
:Q	quit
ZZ	quit
\33\33	quit

▼

This Chapter in Review

▲ The **screen** utility allows you to open multiple windows and applications on a dumb terminal. You can switch between these windows, and you can transfer information between them.

▲ The **calctool** calculator is an improvement on the standard **xcalc** program included with the X Window System. It's also set up differently than the calculators that swear some sort of allegiance to the Hewlett-Packard-type calculators.

▲ Type A personalities can always know what time it is, thanks to **swisswatch** and **xc_clock**.

▲ The **less** command is intended as a substitute for the **more** and **page** commands, allowing you more control over the process of scrolling through a document. Many of the scrolling functions in **less** are the same as those found in **vi**, so any familiarity with **vi** is a plus in this situation. In addition, **less** is very flexible, which means you can assign your own keys to the scrolling functions.

▪ CHAPTER NINE ▪
Linux

The concept of UNIX freeware and shareware extends to versions of the operating system itself. For the price of a CD-ROM, you can have your own version of UNIX, ready to install on a CD-ROM. This chapter covers Linux and FreeBSD, two UNIX freeware titles, as well as the following topics:

- ▲ UNIX as freeware
- ▲ Introducing Linux
- ▲ What you'll need to run Linux
- ▲ Acquiring Linux
- ▲ Installing Linux
- ▲ Introducing FreeBSD

UNIX Itself as Freeware

UNIX, in many ways, began life as freeware, although that wasn't the term used at the time. Since AT&T was prohibited from entering the computer field, UNIX was essentially given away.

That tradition is still strong in the UNIX world—even to the point of some versions of UNIX themselves. In fact, some of you may be using freeware or considering its use through one of the popular freely available PC-based UNIX workalikes available. They are *workalikes* because they technically aren't UNIX (indeed, they make no claims for total UNIX compatibility), but for the vast majority of situations this shouldn't make a difference. And they are much cheaper than the hundreds of dollars you can expect to pay for SCO UNIX or Novell's UnixWare.

With all this in mind, what can you expect from a UNIX workalike on the PC? Well, you can expect full support of the UNIX command set. You can expect most of the standard UNIX utilities. You can expect a stable programming environment. And you don't have to give up a thing when it comes to graphics—you'll have access to the X Window System, and you can purchase OSF/Motif from third parties if you're so inclined. But you can also expect minimal or even nonexistent support. And you can expect a demanding operating system that will expose every hardware flaw in your computer system.

Perhaps the leading PC UNIX workalike is Linux (pronounced *lih-nux*, according to developer Linus Torvalds), which has garnered a ton of attention among folks who are shopping for a low-cost UNIX workalike for their home computers. Linux was designed as a stripped-down UNIX clone and has been available for several years.

And, for all practical purposes, you won't know that you're not using the "real" UNIX. In fact, the following features that are available as part of Linux are also found in commercial UNIX releases:

▲ X Window System implementation through XFree86 2.1
▲ MIME and Andrew multimedia mail
▲ Full support of the UNIX command set

▲   Two versions of **emacs**

▲   The GNU C/C++ compiler

▲   Other GNU utilities

▲   **L E A R N   M O R E   A B O U T**   ▲

You can refer back to Chapters 2 and 3 for more on GNU utilities.

What Hardware Will You Need to Run Linux?

On a basic level, this is easy to answer: a PC. However, past that, there's a wide range of options available, so the question is best answered by breaking down requirements into components.

This is technical

Welcome to the brave world of PC hardware. If you've been spoiled on Sun workstations and think that it would be kinda cool to mess around with Linux at home, you're in for an adventure.

Processor

Any PC with a 386, 486, or Pentium processor should have no problems with Linux. A math coprocessor is not required, although one is recommended (especially for 386 users). With 486 and Pentium prices falling from the sky as this book was written, don't mess around with a 386-based PC unless you get it dirt-cheap.

Bus

Linux currently supports ISA, EISA, and VESA Local Bus architectures. The Micro Channel Architecture (MCA) found in most IBM PS/2 models is not supported.

Memory

There's one thing to remember about any computer—the more memory the better. And, like any operating system, Linux is happiest when it has lots of memory. However, Linux (unlike OS/2 or Microsoft *Windows*) operates pretty well with only 4 megabytes of RAM if you're running in text mode, while you'll need a minimum of 8MB of RAM if you're using the X Window System. (12MB is recommended.) In theory, you can use Linux on a 2MB PC, but this isn't a pretty sight.

Hard Disk

Again, the bigger the hard disk, the better. In theory, you could run Linux in only 10MB of hard-disk space, but this is an exceedingly frugal installation. You're better off planning to use 100MB or so for a Linux partition, even though the documentation recommends 60–80MB. (UNIX programs tend to eat up hard-disk space rapidly.)

Almost every hard-disk-controller format should work with Linux, including IDE, RLL, MFM, and most SCSI drives.

Graphics Card

In theory, if your graphics card works under DOS, it should work under Linux. (Remember, the requirements for running a text interface aren't too stringent.) However, the reality is a little different when it comes to running the X Window System in the form of XFree86. XFree86 supports most popular PC graphics cards in a variety of graphics modes (CGA, EGA, VGA, SuperVGA), but there are some specific graphics cards that aren't supported except on an experimental level (for instance, users of Diamond graphics cards will have to make do with an beta driver).

Other Operating Systems

You can have multiple operating systems on your hard drive; unlike other versions of UNIX for the PC, Linux doesn't need to be the first operating system installed on the boot hard drive. When you install Linux, the installation procedure will ask if you want to include support for multiple operating systems.

Linux also allows you to mount partitions from another operating system. For example, you could configure a DOS partition as merely a directory of the root directory. This process occurs when you install Linux.

Floppy Drive

During installation you'll need a single floppy drive (1.44MB 3.5-inch drive or 1.2MB 5.25-inch drive) for booting Linux. The size of the drive matters in the installation process; you don't want to be specifying a 1.44MB drive when your boot floppy drive is really a 1.2MB 5.25-inch drive.

CD-ROM Drive

Linux doesn't actually deal with the CD-ROM drive per se; instead, it communicates with the SCSI card that drives the CD-ROM. Though there is some limited support for a non-SCSI CD-ROM interface, you'll really want to play it safe and go with a SCSI card and a SCSI CD-ROM drive.

Board/drive combos prices have really dropped over the last six months, so you won't go broke buying a good combination.

Obtaining Linux

Linux is a different beast than the other freeware and shareware utilities covered in this book. Linux, as a source-code entity, is graciously given away to the world. Others, including small companies and CD-ROM vendors, take this source code and then shape it into a format that you can more easily install on your PC. Without this customization, installing Linux is a pain, especially if you're not familiar with PC conventions—so Linux, as a result, is not included on the accompanying CD-ROM.

The advice is to work with a CD-ROM vendor to order Linux on a CD-ROM, with all of the installation tools, as well as the bells and whistles (**emacs**, **cslip**, **XFree86**) that are too complicated to coordinate by casual users. When you buy from a third party, you're also entitled to some support via electronic mail or telephone—and more than likely you're going to appreciate this support at one time or another. Vendors include:

▲ **Trans-Ameritech**, 2342A Walsh Ave., Santa Clara, CA 95051. 408/727-3883. Includes the Slackware distribution, which works very well.

▲ **Walnut Creek CD-ROM**, 4041 Pike Lane, Suite D-854, Concord, CA 94520. 510/674-0783. *orders@cdrom.com*.

You're not going to go broke buying a CD-ROM from these folks; generally speaking, you can buy a CD-ROM for less than $50, including shipping and handling.

This is technical

Installing Linux will depend on the version you have. The CD-ROM should contain installation instructions in the root directory. CD-ROMs from the aforementioned vendors will be in the ISO-9660 format with the Rock Ridge Extensions, which means that the files can be read either by a PC or UNIX CD-ROM drive.

▼

You can install Linux from diskettes or from the CD-ROM. Installing by diskette is a pain; the procedure involves copying directories from the CD-ROM onto individual diskettes and then running through the installation process.

The preferred method, however, is to install from the CD-ROM. To do this, you'll need to make two diskettes and boot your PC from those diskettes. If you've got DOS installed on your PC, you can use the install program from the CD-ROM.

Preparing Your PC for Linux Installation

The best-case scenario would have you install Linux on a virgin PC, with very little installed on the hard drive. That means backing up any files and directories to floppy or tape, so that they can be reinstalled after you reconfigure your hard drive.

You'll also want to create a boot diskette containing DOS, although you can do this on any PC. To do so, you can format a diskette and install the operating system at the same time with the following DOS command:

```
C:\DOS> FORMAT A: /S
```

This diskette will be needed if you somehow wreck your hard drive and need to get back to DOS. (This step is not mentioned in the Linux documentation, but you'll find that it can be a lifesaver.) You'll also want to copy the **FDISK.EXE** and **FORMAT.COM** commands from the **/DOS** directory.

This is technical

If you're not familiar with PC and MS-DOS conventions, take a time to familiarize yourself with how a PC backs up information and partitions hard drives. After you've backed up your important data, you can go ahead and reconfigure your hard disk using **FDISK**.

The Linux version of **fdisk** is different than the MS-DOS version, **FDISK.EXE**. Don't use the Linux **fdisk** command to set up MS-DOS or OS/2 partitions.

The DOS **FDISK** command allows you to change the partitions on a hard drive. When you change the size of a partition, you're also essentially removing the existing data from that partition. (There are ways to work around this if you own the *Norton Utilities*, but it's still a process fraught with danger.)

If the DOS partition contains important data, you'll want to create a backup on diskette or tape drive.

If you create a DOS partition and a Linux partition, you can then run both operating systems.

How large should you make each partition? Linux tends to be more demanding when it comes to hard-disk space. On a 212MB hard drive, for example, you'll probably want to give Linux 150MB or so; this will give you enough room for Linux, and it also gives you enough room (just barely) on the DOS partition to run *Windows*.

After you've partitioned the drive, you can go ahead and create the **boot** and **root** floppies from the Linux CD-ROM, following the instructions on the CD-ROM. (The Slackware distribution includes a program that guides you through this procedure.) You're then ready to boot Linux. Follow the instructions on the screen, which will tell you how to login and what program to run to fully install Linux.

FreeBSD

An alternative to Linux is a member of the 386BSD family (386BSD, FreeBSD, and Net386). These are 32-bit operating systems that claim full compliance with the BSD 4.3 version of UNIX. While there are differences between the three (the full history of this software-development process would be akin to a soap opera), your best bet—especially if you're a UNIX beginner—is FreeBSD. According to information distributed by the 386BSD development team, FreeBSD is a cleaned-up version of 386BSD, with many updated utilities in the system updated: "This system [FreeBSD] is not quite as leading edge as NetBSD and is intended to be used as a stable operating environment. The emphasis seems to be on better packaging and improved operation." (Does this mean that NetBSD is intended to be used as an unstable operating environment?)

This is technical

The minimum hardware configuration for FreeBSD is a 386-based PC with a graphics card, 2MB of RAM, and a 20MB hard disk. Again, this is a minimum; a more realistic assessment would be 8MB of RAM and a 100MB-plus hard disk.

You'll want to look at working with a CD-ROM vendor to order a CD-ROM containing FreeBSD.

This Chapter in Review

- ▲ The concept of UNIX freeware and shareware can be extended to the operating system itself, as very ambitious programmers have created UNIX workalikes that run on Intel-based PCs.

- ▲ The workalikes, technically speaking, aren't truly UNIX. But they work closely enough to how UNIX works—close enough for the vast majority of UNIX users.

- ▲ The leading freeware version of UNIX is Linux.

- ▲ Linux has been available for several years and is considered to be a stable implementation.

- ▲ Linux contains many features found in commercial software, including electronic-mail support, the GNU C compiler, and GNU **emacs**.

- ▲ Source code for Linux is freely distributed. Third-party vendors then take this source and make it more usable for the average user.

- ▲ Because most users will appreciate this extra value, Linux was not included on the accompanying CD-ROM. Instead, you're encouraged to seek out a CD-ROM vendor that can sell you Linux on a CD-ROM (typically for under $50) and support the product once you've bought it.

- ▲ FreeBSD is another freeware version of UNIX .

▪ APPENDIX A ▪
For More Information

This book is only the beginning of the journey, should you desire to advance your working knowledge of UNIX. This appendix lays out further sources of information.

Printed Documentation

If the documentation that came with computer systems were any good, there would be no reason for a book like this. Have you browsed through the documentation that came with your UNIX system? Ouch.

This documentation serves its purpose: To provide valuable information for the system administrator. The purpose of this documentation is not to provide illumination for the end user.

While some system-specific information can be found only in the documentation, the vast amount of it is technical information that is geared toward the advanced user. Approach the documentation with a grain of salt: Don't feel inadequate if you don't understand it fully.

Online-Manual Pages

One of the neater UNIX commands is **man**, which displays information about UNIX commands.

There's not a lot to the **man** command (as you'll see from Table A.1, the Command Reference for the **man** command)—essentially, it displays an *online-manual page* about specific UNIX commands. It will not display information about practices and procedures, nor will it display information about specific UNIX topics, like *multitasking* or *processes*. Still, it's quite useful for displaying a *lot* of information about specific commands.

Unfortunately, the **man** command is not fully implemented on some UNIX system, and not at all on other UNIX systems. If you have it, great; if not, lobby your system administrator.

For more information on the **man** command itself (and assuming you have access to it, of course), use the following command line:

```
$ man man
```

TABLE A.1. COMMAND REFERENCE FOR THE MAN COMMAND

man *command*

Purpose
The **man** command displays the online-manual page for a command.

Options
None.

Books

As you can tell by a visit to your local bookstore, there are a ton of titles devoted to the UNIX operating system. However, when you start looking at the titles and the tables of contents, you realize that most of them are meant for advanced users and/or system administrators. By contrast, the book in your hands is one of the few books devoted to anyone other than advanced users and/or system administrators, and perhaps the only one devoted only to the UNIX neophyte.

At this point in your UNIX education, though, you may be ready to move on to more advanced tomes. Here are some titles that should aid you in your higher education pursuits.

General UNIX Titles

UNIX Fundamentals: UNIX Basics. Kevin Reichard, MIS:Press, 1994. This book is the first in this series, and it lays out the basics of UNIX usage. If you're still puzzled by some aspects of UNIX usage, this is a good place to start.

UNIX Fundamentals: UNIX for DOS and Windows Users. Kevin Reichard, MIS:Press, 1994. The second in the UNIX Fundamentals series, this book compares specific tasks within the UNIX operating system for that DOS and *Windows* users.

UNIX Fundamentals: UNIX Communications and Networking. Kevin Reichard and David Burnette, MIS:Press, 1994. The skinny on UNIX networking and communications, ranging to basic network commands (such as **who**) to Internet usage.

Teach Yourself UNIX. Kevin Reichard and Eric F. Johnson, MIS:Press, 1992. This introduction to the UNIX operating system is meant for a more advanced computer user, but still has enough details for the learning beginner. Most of the commands listed in this work are more fully explained in *Teach Yourself UNIX*, while the underlying concepts of UNIX are explained in depth.

UNIX in Plain English. Kevin Reichard and Eric F. Johnson, MIS:Press, 1994. This reference works focuses on in-depth explanations of the important UNIX commands. Definitely the book to be sitting next to your terminal for a quick reference.

X Window System Titles

Using X. Eric F. Johnson and Kevin Reichard, MIS:Press, 1992. This book explains the basics of X Window System usage and configuration. While X Window can be complex, even a beginner is able to handle the very elementary configuration details, as explained in this book.

The UNIX System Administrator's Guide to X. Eric F. Johnson and Kevin Reichard, 1994, M&T Books. Written for someone who worked full-time with UNIX, this book can still be useful for someone not administering a UNIX system.

▼

Online Sources

As you might expect from a computer system with networking built in, there are many online resources you can tap. The greatest amount of information is carried over the Usenet.

Usenet UNIX Newsgroups

The Usenet is a close cousin to the Internet, which was discussed in Chapter 5. The Usenet, however, contains only newsgroups devoted to the discussion of specific topics. Be warned that many of the newsgroups are geared toward experts of one sort or another, and that some may feel that participation by a UNIX neophyte is not exactly welcome.

Asking a general question of a set of UNIX experts is usually met by disdain, rudeness, and techie arrogance. (The exception is the *comp.unix.questions* newsgroup, which is designed specifically for beginners.) If you choose to participate in a specialized topic, you're on your own; the advice from these quarters is to monitor the newsgroups and pick up useful knowledge in that fashion. (In fact, many of the newsgroup feature messages called FAQs, or Frequently Asked Questions. You'll want to pay special attention to messages with this heading.) General questions are best asked of your system administrator or other UNIX users in your area.

There are many newsgroups on the Usenet devoted to UNIX topics. The list in Table A.2 comes directly from a regular compilation of Usenet newsgroups. However, be warned that Table A.2 comprises only a sampling of other UNIX-related newsgroups; other more obscure or specialized newsgroups have been omitted.

TABLE A.2 USENET NEWSGROUPS RELATING TO UNIX.

NEWSGROUP	PURPOSE
comp.unix.admin	Administering a UNIX-based system
comp.unix.advocacy	Arguments for and against UNIX
comp.unix.aix	A discussion of the IBM version of UNIX
comp.unix.aux	A discussion of the Apple Macintosh version of UNIX
comp.unix.bsd	A discussion of Berkeley Software Distribution UNIX
comp.unix.dos-under-unix	A discussion of MS-DOS running under UNIX
comp.unix.large	A discussion of UNIX on mainframes and in large networks
comp.unix.misc	Miscellaneous topics
comp.unix.osf.osf1	A discussion of the Open Software Foundation's OSF/1
comp.unix.pc-clone.16bit	A discussion of UNIX on 80286 architectures
comp.unix.pc-clone.32bit	A discussion of UNIX on 80386 and 80486 architectures
comp.unix.programmer	Q&A for people programming under UNIX
comp.unix.questions	UNIX neophytes group
comp.unix.shell	Using and programming UNIX shells
comp.unix.sys5.r4	A discussion of System V Release
comp.unix.ultrix	A discussion of DEC's Ultrix

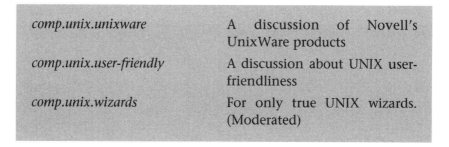

comp.unix.unixware	A discussion of Novell's UnixWare products
comp.unix.user-friendly	A discussion about UNIX user-friendliness
comp.unix.wizards	For only true UNIX wizards. (Moderated)

CompuServe

There are hundreds of forums on CompuServe, but an especially friendly forum for UNIX beginners is the UNIX Forum. Topics in this forum include: Forum Info/General, New to UNIX, Communications, Networking, Applications, UNIX OS Topics, DOS under UNIX, and GUI and X Window. This forum also contains software libraries. (To get to the UNIX Forum, type **GO UNIX**.)

In addition, there are forums maintained by several UNIX vendors that specialize in PC versions of UNIX, and the users on these forums generally have one foot in the DOS world and one foot in the UNIX world. If you need to combine the two worlds, you might want to check out the UnixWare (**GO UNIXWARE**) or SCO (**GO SCO**) forums for some advice and pertinent software libraries.

▲ L E A R N   M O R E   A B O U T ▲

And don't forget the existence of CompuServe forums dedicated to certain portions of UNIX usage. For instance, there's an Internet forum (GO INET) that you might find useful if you want to follow up on Chapter 4.

▪ APPENDIX B ▪
CD-ROM Contents

Here are the contents of the accompanying CD-ROM, listed by directory. In most cases an Internet location is also listed. This isn't to say that these are the *only* locations these files can be found on the Internet—it just means that these are among the handiest. If you want to find alternative locations, you can use the **archie** or **xarchie** utilities discussed in Chapter 4 to perform the search.

Chapter 2: GNU Emacs

PROGRAM	FILENAME
emacs	emacs_19.tar

*Internet location: **prep.ai.mit.edu**, in the **/pub/gnu** directory.*

Chapter 3: Other GNU Software

PROGRAM	FILENAME
GNU C compiler	gcc_2_6.tar
Bison	bison122.tar
Make	make_371.tar
Gzip	gzip1_2.tar
Bourne again shell	bash_1_1.tar
Groff	groff_1_.tar
Text utilities	textutil_tar
NetFax	fax_3_2.tar
Calc	calc_202.tar
Gnuplot	gnuplot.tar
File utilities	fileutil.tar
Diff utilities	diffutil.tar
Shell commands	shutil.tar
Grep replacements	grep_2_0.tar
Find	find_3_8.tar
Uuencode	uuencod_tar
Ghostscript	ghostscr.tar
Gawk	gawk2_15.tar
Gnuchess	gnuchess.tar
Gnugo	gnugo_1_.tar

Internet location for all of the above: **prep.ai.mit.edu**, *in the* **/pub/gnu** *directory.*

Ispell	ispell3_.tar

Internet location: **ftp.cs.ucla.edu**, *in the* **/pub/i-spell3.1** *directory.*

Chapter 4: Freeware Internet Utilities

PROGRAM   FILENAME

Elm   elm2_4.tar

*Internet location: **nigel.msen.com**, in the /pub/packages/mail directory.*

Elm (X Window)   xelm.tar

*Internet location: **ftp.x.org**, in the /contrib/applications directory.*

Archie   archie.tar

*Internet location: **ftp.cs.mcgill.ca**, in the **pub/archie** directory.*

Xarchie   xarchie.tar

*Internet location: **ftp.cs.mcgill.ca**, in the /pub/archie directory.*

Gopher   gopher2.tar

*Internet location: **boombox.micro.umn.edu**, in the /pub/gopher/Unix directory.*

Xgopher   xgopher.tar

*Internet location: **boombox.micro.umn.edu**, in the /pub/gopher/Unix directory.*

Mosaic   xmosaic2.tar

*The version of Mosaic on the CD-ROM is from **ftp.x.org**, in the /contrib directory.*

tkWWW   tkwww_0.tar

*Internet location: **ftp.x.org**, in the /contrib directory.*

CHAPTER 4 CONTINUED

PROGRAM   **FILENAME**

Chimera   **chimera.tar**

*Internet location: **ftp.cs.unlv.edu**, in the **/pub/chimera** directory.*

Lynx   **lynx2_3.tar**

*Internet location: **ftp2.cc.ukans.edu**, in the **/pub/WWW/lynx** directory. (This directory also contains precompiled binaries for Sun 4, AIX, OSF, VAX, and Ultrix.)*

Viola for X   **viola940.tar**

*Internet location: **ftp.ora.com**, in the **/pub/www/viola** directory.*

MidasWWW   **midaswww.tar**

*Internet location: **freehep.scri.fsu.edu**, in the **/freehep/net-working_email_news/midas** directory.*

perlWWW   **perlwww.tar**

*Internet location: **ftp.x.org**, in the **/R5contrib** directory.*

xvnews   **xvnews.tar**

*Internet location: **ftp.x.org**, in the **/R5contrib** directory.*

rn   **rn.tar**

*Internet location: **ftp.psi.com**, in the **/src** directory.*

xrn   **xrn6_17.tar**

*Internet location: **ftp.x.org**, in the **/R5contrib** directory.*

Chapter 5: Image-Editing Tools

PROGRAM	FILENAME
Xgrab	xgrabsc_.tar
Xv	

*Internet location: **ftp.x.org**, in the /R5contrib directory.*

PROGRAM	FILENAME
Pbmplus	
Xv	xv3_01.tar

*Internet location: **ftp.x.org**, in the /R5contrib directory.*

Chapter 6: Games

PROGRAM	FILENAME
Xtetris	xtetris_2tar

*Internet location: **ftp.x.org**, in the /R5contrib directory.*

PROGRAM	FILENAME
Nethack	nethack.tar

*Internet location: **prep.ai.mit.edu**, in the /pub/gnu directory.*

PROGRAM	FILENAME
Xmahjongg	xmahjohn.tar

*Internet location: **gatekeeper.dec.com**, in the
/.b/usenet/comp.sources.x directory.*

PROGRAM	FILENAME
Xsol	xsol.c

Chapter 7: Communications Tools

PROGRAM	FILENAME
Pcomm	pcomm_shitar

Internet location: *ftp.cecer.army.mil*, in the */pcomm* directory.

Kermit	kermit.tar

Internet location: *ftp.psi.com*, in the */src* directory.

Rzsz (zmodem)	rzsz9202.tar

Internet location: *nigel.msen.com*, in the */pub/packages/utils* directory.

Chapter 8: Miscellaneous UNIX and X Tools

PROGRAM	FILENAME
Screen	screen_3.tar

Internet location: *prep.ai.mit.edu*, in the */pub/gnu* directory.

Calctool	calctool.tar

Internet location: *sun.soe.clarkson.edu*, in the */pub/src* directory.

Swisswatch	swisswat.tar

Internet location: *ftp.x.org*, in the */R5contrib* directory.

PROGRAM   **FILENAME**

Xc_clock   **xc_clock.tar**

Internet location: **ftp.cae.wisc.edu**, *in the* **/hpux9/X11R5/Demos** *directory.*

Less   **less_177.tar**

Internet location: **nigel.msen.com**, *in the* **/pub/packages/utils** *directory.*

Xless   **xless1_7.tar**

Internet location: **ftp.x.org**, *in the* **/contrib/applications** *directory*

▪ APPENDIX C ▪
Using the Accompanying CD-ROM

Now that you've seen a cross section of UNIX freeware and shareware explained, you'll want to take a crack at actually installing it and using it.

One Size Does Not Fit All

The best thing about the UNIX operating system is that it runs on a wide variety of platforms in a number of usable configurations.

The worst thing about the UNIX operating system is that it runs on a wide variety of platforms in a number of usable configurations.

Though UNIX is pretty much the same—at least when it comes to basic commands and structures—across different machines from different vendors, the same cannot be said when it comes to software installations. Since most vendors like to combine proprietary features with their idea of an "open systems" platform like UNIX, the result is a UNIX world where everyone's system is a little different, everyone's file structures are a little different, and everyone's software-development environment is a little different.

▼

The message? There's no "one" way to install the programs on the accompanying CD-ROM. Instead, you're going to have to work with the programs, their documentation (which, by and large, is very good), and your system administrator.

Indeed, if you have a good system administrator, it should take them no time at all to get the programs on the CD up and running. To get you started, the various installation notes are collected in this chapter for your easy perusal. Past that, however, you're on your own.

Information About The Programs

The accompanying CD-ROM contains the programs discussed in this book. They are arranged by chapter; for instance, since the discussion of **emacs** occurs in Chapter 2, the **emacs** file is contained in the **chapter2** directory.

The files on the CD-ROM are exactly the same as you'll find them on the Internet. Because smaller files are easier to move around and work with, they've been left in their compressed, archived format.

However, one concession was made to the quirks of the UNIX world. To avoid problems with short and long names, the files are written in a DOS-style eight-dot-three format, though in a UNIX **tar** format.

▼

This is technical

You don't need the Rock Ridge Extensions to read this CD-ROM on your system; all you need is the ability to read ISO 9660-formatted CD-ROMs. The UNIX world—including Linux, UnixWare, and SCO users—should be fine.

Because these files are in the UNIX **tar** format, you're going to need to unarchive them. In addition, you're also going to need to uncompress the files, if need be.

Running Make and Imake

Unfortunately, you're going to need to know a little about UNIX software installation if you want to install most of this software. UNIX relies on a command called **make** to install much software, while the X Window System relies on a command called **imake**, which does the same thing.

Command

Each application will come with one or more files usually named **Makefile**. This file (there's usually one in each source-code directory) contains the rules to build a particular application. Armed with these rules, and presuming the rules are properly configured for your system, you can build an X application by simply invoking **make** on the command line. With this, make will follow the rules in the **Makefile** and generally compile each source-code module in the current directory. Some **Makefiles** are much more complex than this, of course, especially for X programs.

If all goes well, you shouldn't ever have to read the automatically generated **Makefile**. You should just be able to type **make** on the command line and the program should load.

▼

▼

Imake is a program that generates a **Makefile** tuned to your system's setup. **Imake** uses its own rules and builds a **Makefile** from a template file (which describes your system's setup) and a set of rules for building a program. You use **Imake** to install new X program libraries, and (where this book is concerned) to install the free X applications that you can get from CompuServe, from Usenet newsgroups, and from various program archive sites on the Internet.

Contacting the FSF

Some of the programs on the CD-ROM are from the Free Software Foundation, which produces more than just these programs. If you want more information about the FSF and its activities, you can use **ftp** to *prep.ai.mit.edu*, or you can use more mundane means:

> Free Software Foundation
> 675 Massachusetts Ave.
> Cambridge, MA 02139
> 617/876-3296 (voice)
> 617/492-9057 (fax)
> *gnu@prep.ai.mit.edu*

▼

▪ GLOSSARY ▪

Not all of these terms are used in this book. However, as you delve into the world of UNIX, you'll run across these terms often.

absolute pathname	The full name of a file, from the root directory on through each subdirectory.
account	Information about your UNIX usage, such as your username and the way your terminal is configured.
address	The name of a computer on the network or the name of the entire computer system, used in communications and electronic mail.
anonymous ftp	Logging on a remote system anonymously to retrieve files (that is, logging in a system without having an account already set up on the system); this method involves limited access to the remote system.
append	Attach characters to the end of an existing file.
application	A program that perform a specific task, such as a text editor or a database manager.
archive	A file that can contain one or more files, serving as a backup (usually on tape) to files on a hard drive.
arguments	Additions to a command that slightly change the result of the command, either by adding options or specifying filenames.

ASCII	American Standard Code for Information Interchange; a standard format used to store basic alphabetic characters and numerals in a way that any computer—running UNIX or another operating system—can read the file.
background	The state where commands are run without the full attention and resources of the system; when the commands finish running the user is notified. Background commands are run from a command line that ends with an ampersand (&).
Bourne shell	see *shell*.
C	Programming language that serves as a basis of UNIX; in addition, most UNIX programs are written in C or its successor, C++.
C shell	see *shell*.
command	A direct instruction to the computer system.
command line	The combination of a command and any arguments to the command.
command prompt	A specific character used by a specific shell in conjunction with the cursor to tell you that the system is ready for a command.
compiler	Program that turns C source code and other related files into executable programs.
compressed file	A file that has been shrunk so it can be transferred more quickly from computer to computer.
current directory	Your current position on the directory tree.
cursor	A blinking line or square on the monitor that tells you that the system is waiting for a command.

▼

default	A state or value assumed when no other is present.
device	A physical device attached to the computer system, such as a modem or tape drive.
directory	The means for storing files or other directories, analogous to a folder in a file cabinet.
DOS	see *MS-DOS*.
electronic mail	The electronic equivalent of mail: text messages sent over the UNIX network, either from within the system or from outside the system.
encryption	A way of encoding a file so that it cannot be read by other users.
environment	Information that determines your UNIX usage and system configuration, as stored in your **.profile** file or set during your computing session.
error message	A message from the computer system informing you that it cannot perform a specific function.
executable file	A file containing a program.
FAQ (Frequently Asked Questions)	A list of commonly asked questions on a specific topic (and their answers, of course) disseminated via the Internet.
field	A vertical column of data from a structured data file, with all of the entries of the same type.
file	The mechanism for storing information on a UNIX system: A set of characters (called bytes) referenced by its filename.
filename	The name for a file.

filesystem	The method used in UNIX to organize files and directories: A root directory contains several subdirectories, and these subdirectories in turn may contain further subdirectories.
foreground	Commands that have the full attention of the system and do not return control of the system to the user until the command is complete. In UNIX, the default is to run commands in the foreground.
freeware	Software created by others and then given away to the computing community at large.
graphical interface	A graphical display on the monitor, with windows, scrollbars, and icons.
group	A defined set of users.
hidden files	UNIX system files that are used for standard housekeeping chores; the filenames begin with a period (.) and are not listed with the **ls** command.
home directory	A directory where your own files are stored, and where you are placed after you login the system.
hostname	The name of your UNIX system.
icon	A graphical representation of a program or file.
inbox	The storage area for electronic mail that has not been read.
Internet	The umbrella name for a group of computer networks that distribute electronic mail and newsgroups around the world.
keyboard	The big thing you type on to provide input to the computer.
Korn shell	see *shell*.

▼

link	A file that serves as a reference to another file. Many users can use the same files, making it appear as though they each have their own copy of the file.
login	To announce your presence to the system by entering your username and password.
login shell	A script, usually contained in **.login**, that contains basic information about your UNIX usage; this script runs every time you login.
logname	The name the UNIX system uses to keep track of you. Also known as *username*.
Meta key	A specified key used in conjunction with other keys to create additional key combinations. On most keyboards, the **Alt** key is really the **Meta** key.
monitor	That big ol' thing sitting on your desk that looks like a television on steroids.
multiprocessing	When more than one task can be performed simultaneously by the operating system. UNIX is a *multiprocessing* operating system.
multitasking	When more than one task can be performed simultaneously by the operating system. UNIX is a *multitasking* operating system.
multiuser	When more than one user can be using the same computer system. UNIX is a *multiuser* operating system.
MS-DOS	An operating system used by most PCs.
networking	Connecting one computer system to another computer system by direct wiring or phone lines.

online manual page	Documentation for your system stored within files on the system, accessed with the man command.
operating system	A program that controls all actions of the computer hardware. UNIX is an operating system.
option	Characters that modify the default behavior of a command.
ordinary file	A file that is, well, ordinary, containing data or programs, with no special characters.
OSF/Motif	Created by the Open Software Foundation, Motif is actually many things—but for you, the most important thing is that it defines a look and feel for the graphical interface. Based on the X Window System.
owner	The user with the ability to set permissions for a file.
paging	Memory-management system where entire chunks of the UNIX system's RAM is switched back and forth to the hard disk. This situation occurs when there's not enough RAM to serve the needs of all users.
parent directory	The directory containing a subdirectory.
password	A unique set of character that the UNIX system uses to verify your existence when you want to login the system.
permissions	A security tool to determine who can access a file.
pipe	A conduit between two commands, which tells the second command to use the output from the first command as input.

▼

process	Essentially, a program running on the computer.
process ID (PID)	The number assigned by the system to a command.
program	A set of instructions for the computer to carry out.
prompt	See *command prompt*.
redirection	Changing the standard input/output; for instance, saving output to a file instead of printing it to the screen.
relative pathname	A filename in relation to the current directory position.
root directory	The top-most directory on the directory tree; every directory on a UNIX **system** is a subdirectory of the root directory. Indicated in all pathnames as a slash (/).
root user	The user who can do just about anything possible within the UNIX operating system. Also referred to as the **superuser**.
server	A computer that supplies files and services to other computers.
shareware	Software that's distributed over noncommercial channels, such as online services and CD-ROM vendors, where the authors request that you directly send them money should you find the programs useful.
shell	Software that acts as a buffer between you and the operating system. There are many different UNIX shells—the Bourne shell, the Korn shell, and the C shell, for example.

▼

shell script

A text file that serves as a set of instructions for the shell.

special device files

Files that represent physical parts of the UNIX system, such as tape drives or terminals.

standard input/output

The UNIX method of processing commands: The standard input comes from the keyboard, and the output goes to the screen.

states

Different levels that a UNIX system runs in, ranging from a single-user state to a multiuser state.

subdirectories

A directory contained within another directory. In UNIX, every directory is a subdirectory of the root directory.

swapping

Situation where UNIX processes are sent from RAM to a hard disk for temporary storage. This arises because of a shortage of available RAM in the system.

system administrator

Your hero/heroine—the person responsible for running and maintaining the UNIX system.

terminal

A monitor, keyboard, perhaps a mouse, and perhaps a CPU.

text-based interface

An interface where only characters, and not graphics, are used.

text file

A file containing only ASCII characters and no special characters. A text file can be read by any program.

UNIX

An operating system that supports more than one user and can perform more than one command at a time—and, of course, the greatest operating system in the world.

▼

username	The name that the UNIX system uses to keep track of you. Also known as *logname*.
variable	A symbol or character that has different meanings based on context and specific usage.
wildcard	Special characters within a filename that tells the shell to look for all files with similar filenames.
window manager	A program within the X Window System that controls the look and feel of the interface.
working directory	see *current directory*.
workstation	A computer optimized for running UNIX. Sun SPARCstations and IBM RS/6000s are *workstations*.
X terminal	A terminal that runs only the X Window System and draws most of its computing power from the network.
X Window System	Graphical windowing system used for building graphical interfaces, like Motif.
xterm	Popular X Window System program that provides a command-line interface to the UNIX operating system.

▼

▪ INDEX▪

▪ A ▪

▪ B ▪

▪ C ▪

▪ D ▪

▪ E ▪

▪ F ▪

▪ G ▪

▪ **H** ▪

▼

▪ I ▪

▪ K ▪

▪ L ▪

▪ M ▪

▪ N ▪

▪ O ▪

▪ P ▪

▼

■ **X** ■

■ **Z** ■